Can you ever be 100 percent sure that someone you're with is the right one for you?

What qualities should a partner have?

How important is sexual chemistry in a relationship?

Is it possible for a couple to rediscover sexual desire for each other after it has disappeared?

How long should it take to recover from a breakup?

Why do my partner and I fight all the time? How can we stop?

If your partner has an affair, should you just forgive and forget? How do you learn to trust again?

Is there a way to detect symptoms of trouble in your relationship so you can solve the problems before they get too serious?

First comes love, then comes . . . questions? In *Ask Barbara*, bestselling author and renowned relationship expert Barbara De Angelis, Ph.D., spotlights the 100 intimate issues that most often challenge couples in love— and singles searching for the right partner.

With warmth, wisdom, and compassion, she draws from her own experiences as well as those of the thousands of men and women who attend her standing-room-only seminars to deliver all the advice you need—to create a love that will last forever!

"Barbara has the advice guaranteed to make your love life soar."
—*Complete Woman*

Also
by
Barbara
De Angelis

The Real Rules
Real Moments® for Lovers
Real Moments®
Are You the One for Me?
Secrets About Men Every Woman Should Know
How to Make Love All the Time

Barbara De Angelis, Ph.D.

ASK BARBARA

The 100 Most-Asked Questions About Love, Sex, and Relationships

Island
BOOKS

ISLAND BOOKS
Published by
Dell Publishing
a division of
Bantam Doubleday Dell Publishing Group, Inc.
1540 Broadway
New York, New York 10036

ISBN: 0-440-22428-4

Reprinted by arrangement with Delacorte Press

Printed in the United States of America

Published simultaneously in Canada

January 1998

10   9   8   7   6   5   4   3   2   1

OPM

I humbly dedicate this book
To my beloved Teacher,
Whose Light has kindled my own,
Whose Love has made me whole,
And Who, in a sublime and miraculous instant,
Answered all my questions
By revealing the Truth to me.

Acknowledgments

Special thanks to the following people:

Carole Baron, publisher of Delacorte, for your continued trust and invaluable support of me and my work.

Tracy Devine, my wonderful editor, for your patience, your praise, and for always seeing the essence of the contribution I'm trying to make.

Harvey Klinger, my literary agent, for always sharing my vision and being there whenever I need you.

Michael and Marlise Karlin, my dear friends, for being true instruments of grace, and bringing me back to where I've always belonged.

Sandy Jolley, my sister in spirit, for instantly recognizing my heart, and being my gentle guardian on the journey.

Martha Mendez Cole, my assistant, for staying on the train with me, even as it goes faster and in new directions, for your loyalty and your love.

Sat-Kaur Khalsa, for your gentle wisdom and supreme clarity as you helped prepare me to receive the magnificent new level of awakening in my life.

Bijou, Shanti and Luna, my beloved animal companions, for your silent devotion, your kisses, and your comforting company beneath my desk while I wrote this book.

Special gratitude to the tens of thousands of men and women who have trusted me with your questions in my seminars, in letters, on the radio, and wherever you find me. I honor you for your courage, your honesty, and your search for the truth.

And most of all, my husband, Jeffrey, for being my best friend, my healer, my light, my inspiration, and for traveling with me along the invisible and sublime road that is leading us Home.

The 100 Most-Asked Question About Love, Sex, and Relationships

Compatibility

Commitment

Communication and Conflict

Sex and Physical Affection

Cheating and Infidelity

PAGE

Breaking Up, Starting Over

Living and Loving

Dear Reader,

Everywhere I go, and I mean *everywhere*, people ask me questions about their love life. I can be eating dinner in a restaurant, standing in line for a movie, sitting on an airplane, or walking down the street—it doesn't matter—and someone will approach me with a question they're desperate to get answered. I've talked to men and women about the most intimate details of their relationships in the strangest of places, from the dressing room of a department store, to the galley of a jumbo jetliner crossing the Atlantic in the middle of the night, to a hiking trail in the California mountains, to the restroom of a museum in Paris.

What do people ask me? ANYTHING!!! I've had a salesperson ask me if I thought she should stay with her boyfriend even though he was sleeping with his ex-wife . . . while I was buying underwear! I've had a Marine officer roll down his car window and ask me to explain why his girlfriend was mad that he went to a friend's bachelor party . . . while his vehicle drove alongside mine at fifty miles an hour! I've had a security guard at an airport ask my advice on how he could give his wife an orgasm . . . while he X-rayed my carry-on bags! Then there was the time a cab driver was intent on discovering the secrets of getting women to be attracted to him and (as I discovered later) drove me miles out of my way in order to prolong the ride!

However unusual the circumstances or delicate the questions, most of the time I'm happy to offer my answers to the people who approach me (that is, unless I'm in the middle of chewing a mouthful of food, or trying to have an intimate night out with my husband!!). The reason is simple: I have great respect for anyone who has the honesty and courage to search for the truth about love, sex, and relationships. I believe that most of us need to ask ourselves and the people we love more questions, questions that will help us live with more integrity, love with more success, and move through our days and nights with more peace.

After almost twenty years of teaching about personal and spiritual development, it dawned on me that there were certain questions I kept hearing over and over again, at my seminars, through letters, on call-in radio and television programs. They are the kind of questions that anyone who has ever been in an intimate relationship needs the answers to. They are the questions you've asked yourself when you're lying in bed late at night, the questions your friends call and ask you when they're having a hard time, the questions whose answers you wish you'd had before your first date.

I wrote this book to be like a *"love encyclopedia,"* offering you information in various categories to help you with whatever you're going through at a particular time in your life. You can read the book from beginning to end, or just turn to a section that specifically applies to your issues right now. And whenever you're having an argument with your mate, or when you're wondering how to handle a particular situation in your love life, or when a friend in a romantic crisis calls you up asking for advice, look through the list of questions, turn to that page, and you'll find the answer.

If you've read any of my other books, you know that I believe creating successful relationships takes a lot of commitment and hard work. So obviously, *Ask Barbara* isn't meant to be a cure-all for every personal issue you are faced with in your love life. My hope, though, is that what I've offered you in these pages will help connect you to your own inner wisdom, and guide you to discover the answers that are already waiting for you in your own heart.

In love,

Barbara De Angelis
July 25, 1996
Los Angeles, California

Love
and
Intimacy

1 *How do you convince a workaholic partner to put more time and energy into a marriage?*

I feel like I'm always competing with my husband's job. He's an attorney and works sixty to seventy hours a week, not to mention most weekends, which doesn't leave much time for me and our two boys. When I complain, he argues that he's doing this for us, and points to our lifestyle, which I have to admit, is very luxurious—we have a beautiful home, a boat, a vacation cabin (which we hardly use), and all the money we need. The only thing missing is him! He blows up when I call him a workaholic, and tells me I'm being ungrateful. Is he right? How can I convince him to pay attention to us?

➤➤♥♥♥➤ You're not ungrateful . . . you're just lonely, and with good cause. You can't snuggle up to a checkbook, or hold hands with a share of stock, and neither can your kids. I have a saying: *Marriage is not a noun, it's a verb. It's not something you have, like a house or a car. It is not a piece of paper that proves you are husband and wife. Marriage is a behavior. It is a choice you make over and over again, reflected in the way you treat your partner every day.*

Men tend to define themselves by what they are *doing*, rather than what they are *feeling*, so it's no surprise that your husband has gotten caught up in the "doing more must mean I'm successful" mentality. That's the way society, and perhaps his family background, has trained him. He may feel like he's on a treadmill, running as fast as he can, and he doesn't know *how to* stop. Along with this, he may have other unconscious emotional reasons for working so hard. Some workaholics actually use their business to avoid intimacy and to maintain a sense of control over their lives. After all, it's probably easier for your husband to feel in control when he's doing business than it is when he's interacting with you and your children, and dealing in emotions, needs, and all that amorphous stuff.

Here are a few of my favorite methods to wake up workaholic partners. Whether or not these approaches are effective will depend on how addicted your mate is to the illusion of power and control that work gives him.

1. **Give him some perspective.** Have him close his eyes and imagine that he's at the end of his life, on his deathbed. As he looks back on his life, ask him to share what moments will have made his life truly meaningful. What, in the end, will really matter to him? You can bet he won't say "I can die happily because I closed ten big deals in 1997," or "I feel content with my life because I owned a five-thousand-square-foot house," or even "I feel at peace because I left my children a lot of money." No, the moments that really matter, the moments that will have filled his life with meaning will be moments of love, connection, and sharing.

I call these "real moments," and he probably isn't having enough of them because he's too busy doing the things he has decided are more important. Tell him you want to share more meaningful time with him.

2. **Use fear to scare him into slowing down.** Sometimes this is the only thing that works to snap a guy out of his workaholic stupor. Ask him how he would spend his time if he knew he had only one month left to live. (Trust me, he won't say "I'd work like a dog for twelve hours a day.") Then remind him of some men he knows of who have died at his age, either accidentally or of natural causes. *The truth is, we never know if a day, or a month, or a year will be our last.* We live as if we have all the time in the world, and we don't. Share this anonymous quote with him:

First I was dying to finish high school and start college.
And then I was dying to finish college and start working.
And then I was dying to marry and have children.
And then I was dying for my kids to grow up.
And then I was dying to retire.
And now, I am dying, and suddenly I realize, I forgot to live. . . .

3. *Use guilt as a last resort.* Ask him to imagine what his children will say about him when they are grown. Does he really think they will look back on their childhood as happy because of their big house and expensive toys, and not care that they hardly saw their father? Does he really think that they don't care that he is hardly ever around? All children really want is to feel they matter, that they are important to us. The toys and treats may buy the children's silence now, but when they grow up, they won't even remember what he bought them—they'll only say "I hardly knew my dad." And they will wish he hadn't sacrificed "for their sakes," because whatever he leaves them will never be as valuable as the cherished memory of a good-night story, a game of catch, or the sight of Mommy and Daddy snuggled close together on the couch.

2 Is it natural for the passion to disappear after years of marriage?

My husband and I have been married for eighteen years and are more like best friends than lovers. We have sex very infrequently and have settled into what I would call a "comfortable" relationship. There's a part of me that longs for that passionate emotional connection we used to have, but many of my friends tell me I'm being unrealistic, and that all couples feel this way after years of marriage. Am I expecting too much?

▰❤❤➤ Don't buy into the popular but misinformed attitude that losing romantic attraction to your partner is an inevitable part of marriage. That's like saying becoming unhealthy and having a heart attack is an inevitable part of growing older. Are heart attacks common? Yes—but now we know they are preventable IF you take good care of your body. In the same way, just because it's *common* for many couples to lose the passion in their relationship over time doesn't mean it is *natural*. It all depends on how you take care of your relationship.

Relationships don't just lose their chemistry overnight. It takes years of neglect, not making the marriage a number-one priority, not talking about your needs, not resolving and healing hidden resentments, and not actively learning how to make love work. All these unhealthy emotional habits are what takes a couple from feeling "in love" to feeling like roommates.

I strongly believe that you *do* deserve to have a marriage that grows in love, passion, and connection year after year. Is this realistic, even in an eighteen-year relationship? Yes . . . IF both partners decide to do what it takes to rekindle the passion and learn some of the skills you were never taught about successful loving. *Start by sitting down with your partner, taking his hands, and telling him how much you miss the physical and emotional closeness you used to share. (Believe me, he misses it too!) Without blaming him, tell him you want to work toward transforming your "comfortable" relationship into one that is intimate and exciting. Tell him he deserves more than he's getting, as you do. When you both recommit to learning how to love, and use some of the skills I teach in my books and programs, you'll find renewed levels of communication, closeness, and excitement.*

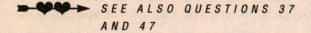 *SEE ALSO QUESTIONS 37 AND 47*

3 If a relationship takes a lot of work, does that mean something is wrong with it?

At times, I find myself wondering whether my wife is my perfect partner, because our relationship doesn't ever seem to be completely effortless and without issues. We love each other very much and have grown tremendously over the past eight years, but it seems we're always "dealing" with something—balancing her needs with mine; learning to ask for what we want; giving each other enough attention, or space. Should it be this complicated?

━━♥♥♥━ Yes! Show me a relationship without conflict and issues and I'll show you a couple that is either dead or in denial! A conscious relationship requires a lot of work, because it asks you to push past the fear that would keep you protected and invulnerable to your partner and, instead, to reveal *all* of you—the giving *and* the selfish part; the forgiving *and* the angry part; the compassionate *and* the blaming part. **In other words, a truly honest, deep, and committed relationship will continually confront you with all the parts of yourself that are not totally loving, and thus will make you uncomfortable as it stretches you beyond the boundaries of your ego.**

Where I think people get stuck is in the erroneous belief that a relationship is always supposed to make you feel good, so if it *feels* bad, it must *be* bad. Actually, it is often during the times when the relationship doesn't feel good that something good is happening: You are being forced to see a part of yourselves or a dynamic between you that is not healthy, so you can change it and make your relationship even stronger. *It may feel like things are falling apart, but actually, they are trying to come more together.* It's at these times when you need to be careful not to misinterpret your difficulties as signs of doom, but rather, opportunities for growth. (This only applies if you are actually with the right person in the first place—see section on compatibility.)

Of course, *both* partners need to be willing to work on themselves and the relationship. And it's essential to share a vision and understanding of the purpose of your relationship, so that when stuff comes up, and it will, you remember what you're doing there in the first place. Here are three understandings I suggest couples adopt:

1. *We have been brought together for the purpose of helping each other grow, and will be each other's teacher.*

2. *Our relationship is a precious gift—it will take us through whatever we need to learn to become more conscious, loving human beings.*

3. *The challenges and difficulties we experience will always illuminate our most needed lessons.*

➡❤❤❤➡ SEE ALSO QUESTION 37

How do you deal with a partner who is a flirt?

My boyfriend of two years is a flirt! He's always staring at other women when we are together, especially certain body parts, and sometimes he even comes on to women right in front of me. When I complain about his behavior, he insists he's just being "friendly," and "joking around," and accuses me of being "insecure" and "jealous." What do you think?

■━♥♥━➤ What I think doesn't count—it's what *you* think and feel that matters, and you already know what that is. You think he's acting like an insensitive jerk, and he is! You don't need me to validate your opinion, but since you asked, I'll add a little something! What your boyfriend is doing is totally disrespectful. I call it "leaking sexual energy." He may not be doing anything physical, but on the astral plane, he's lusting after, undressing, and probably doing much more to other women, and right in front of you no less. His saying it's just "friendly" behavior is like someone whose dog is humping your leg telling you the animal is just being friendly. You know it's much more—you can feel it in your gut.

As for his accusations that you are "insecure" and "jealous," those are buzz words men (and women) often use to control their partner, invalidate their feelings, and make them feel something is wrong with them. Don't fall for it, and don't let him minimize what he's doing to you. This is a problem that needs facing.

See, there's a difference between "noticing" that

another human being is attractive as she walks by, and enjoying the contribution her beauty adds to the world, and, on the other hand, having a wild, ten-second sexual orgy with her in your imagination. The first is *acknowledging* attractiveness; the second is *indulging* in it and, temporarily, forgetting that your sexual commitment is to your partner. And you know when your lover is doing the second, because it feels like he disappeared for ten seconds—and he did.

Now, let me take his side for a moment, because the fact is that unfortunately our society trains and even supports men to behave in this disrespectful manner toward women. It's the old eye-winking, back-slapping boys' club that gives men points for "scoring," and looks the other way on cheating, flirting, etc. So it's possible that your sweetheart *is* a really nice, but misguided, member of the male race who just doesn't realize how his behavior is hurting you. Then again, it's possible that he's *not* a nice guy and couldn't care less about your feelings. That's a distinction only you can make.

Try sharing this information with your boyfriend without blaming him, coming from a more neutral place. See if it helps him understand how hurtful his behavior is to you, and let him know you respect yourself too much to stay in the relationship if the flirting continues.

➡️〰️💚💚💚➡️   SEE ALSO QUESTION 54

5 *How can I stop mothering my husband?*

My husband and I have been married for ten years, and have three small children, but I feel like I have four kids—including him. I find myself treating him like a child because he acts like one. He's always misplacing things, forgetting appointments, and leaving his stuff all over the house. I hate feeling this way, and I know it turns him off, because our sex life is practically nonexistent. How can I stop acting like his mother?

━━❤❤❤➤ Boy, am I glad you asked. Mothering our men is one of the biggest mistakes women make in relationships. The more we treat them like little boys, the more they act like it. They end up resenting us and, eventually, rebelling against us just like they did against Mom at some point. And what's worse, *mothering your mate is the quickest and deadliest way to kill the passion in your love life.* After all—no man wants to sleep with his mother, so if you're acting like her, it's going to be just about impossible to turn him on, unless he has a strange fetish for nagging and scolding.

Now, as a woman, I know how natural it is to mother someone you love. We're trained to do it from the time we are children ourselves. After all, your first and most predominant experience of love was probably associated with your mother, who carried you inside her for nine months, fed you, bathed you, burped you, and powdered your behind. Once you realized you, too, were a female, it was just a mental hop, skip, and jump to treating people you love with a "mothering, nurturing" attitude. There's only one problem—it drives men crazy, reminds them of you know who, and makes them want to leave home all over again.

There are six "Mommy-No-No's" that we do as women:

1. **We act overly helpful by doing things for men that they should be doing for themselves** (choosing his clothes, picking up after him, finding his keys).

2. **We play verbal guessing games with men to try and pull information out of them.** ("You're hungry . . . how about some cereal? No? What about pretzels? Not pretzels? Okay, what if I make you some nice soup?")

3. **We assume men will be absentminded or forgetful and remind them of information they should remember by themselves.** ("Don't forget it's trash night . . ." "Don't forget to pick up milk . . .")

4. **We scold men as if they were children.** ("How many times do I have to tell you to turn off the kitchen lights?")

5. **We take charge of activities that we assume they can't do right.** (Planning trips, taking the kids out to buy clothing.)

6. **We correct and direct them when they don't ask for our help.** (Correcting their memory, offering the "right way" to cook something.)

I know what you're thinking . . . "But he always forgets where he put his keys" . . . "But if I don't do it, it won't get done . . ." Believe me, I've been there. All I can say is that you have much more to lose by behaving motherly than you do by waiting for him to find the keys once in a while. So here are my rules for you to follow if you want to transform yourself from a mother back into a lover:

Rule #1: Stop doing things for your mate that he can do for himself.

Rule #2: Treat him like a competent, reliable person.

Rule #3: Don't speak to him in "Mommy-talk."

Rule #4: Agree on what responsibilities are his in the relationship, and don't take over even if he makes a mistake.

Rule #5: Make a list: "The ways I play Mommy . . ." Read it every day, and give him a copy so he can bust you when you fall off the wagon.

Hang in there, and remember—when you break the mothering habit, you will feel and act more like a woman, and he will feel and act more like a man.

How can I help my partner break through the emotional barriers she put up because of her painful childhood?

My wife had a very tough childhood, lots of physical and verbal abuse and very little love. The result is that she has locked herself behind thick emotional walls, and no matter what I do, I can't get through to her. I know she loves me, but she has a hard time showing it and is very withdrawn. Is it possible for someone like this to ever open up? What can I do to break through her walls?

I'm going to say something you may not want to hear: *It's not your job to break through to her. It's not your job to rescue her. It's her job to rescue herself.* That doesn't mean you can't be a part of her healing process, but that can only happen if she decides she wants to break free from her emotional prison.

Perhaps, like many of us who have loved someone in emotional pain, and wanted desperately to save that person, you haven't asked your wife the most important questions: **Do you *want* to change? Do you want to open up emotionally? Are you willing to do whatever it takes, counseling, reading, seminars, to heal yourself of the emotional damage from your childhood?**

Whether your marriage works or not lies in her answers to these questions. If she wants to heal herself, and is willing to take action to do so, then you have a chance. *But if she won't, or can't start a journey*

of recovery, you will need to face a very heartbreaking but
necessary fact—your wife may be emotionally incapable of
having the kind of healthy relationship you want, at least
right now, and perhaps for a long time to come. Some
people truly are too wounded, too damaged to love
fully and freely. And ironically, your pressuring your
wife to open up and let you in may actually make her
feel even worse about herself and more like a failure
than if she were in a less demanding relationship, or
even lived alone.

While you're asking her the questions I mentioned, you need to ask yourself some too, because it's
no accident that you are in this kind of relationship
and are acting as a rescuer. *Rescueholics tend to become*
involved with partners they feel compelled to help, whom
they feel sorry for. This almost always goes back to your
own unfinished emotional business from childhood.
Maybe there was someone you couldn't rescue, but
wanted to, like an abused mom, an alcoholic dad, an
ailing sibling. Or maybe the person you wanted someone else to rescue was yourself, so you're acting it out
as an adult. Do some emotional work on your own issues, because you may "need" her to be messed up in
order to run out your own patterns.

Someone once said that you can't force a flower
to open its petals before it's time. Find the courage to
ask your wife if she's ready to work on loving you
the way you need to be loved, and know that the
truth will set you both free.

7 Is it possible to "fall back in love" with someone after years of feeling dead and disinterested?

I've been married for twenty-eight years, and for the last ten, I've felt numb toward my partner. We've discussed divorce, but neither of us really wants to go out and start dating at this point in our lives. Is it possible for us to fall back in love again, or should we just accept the fact that our marriage is over?

━━❤❤❤➤ Yes, it's possible to fall back in love again, or more accurately, to break through the numbness you are both feeling and rediscover the love that is still there underneath. If you're a couple (and I'd bet anything you are) who never worked on maintaining the intimacy in your relationship, avoided major confrontation, suppressed unpleasant emotions, and didn't talk about your feelings, then of course you are feeling numb. *You've spent years becoming experts at numbing yourselves to the little things, and now you're wondering where the love went.* It may still be there in hibernation, underneath all the other frozen emotions.

It sounds to me like you are both not only numb to one another, but numb period. You aren't interested in dating or starting your love life over again, and I'll bet you feel kind of tired and blasé about everything. This could be a major turning point in your life, a moment where you look at one another and say, *"I'm tired of feeling this tired of everything . . .*

I'm tired of feeling numb . . . I'm ready to make some changes."

The first step is to break through that numbness by confronting some of the issues that are sure to be lurking beneath the surface. You won't be able to do this on your own—you'll need help, and I suggest you find a well-trained therapist or marriage counselor who has an excellent reputation for helping couples in trouble. If you don't get the results you want, try someone else, read books, attend seminars, etc. *You won't be able to tell if your marriage can be saved until you try everything.* Then, if you decide it's over, you can do so knowing you made every attempt to resurrect the relationship.

Here's something to give you some hope: I've personally worked with thousands of couples who believed they were on the verge of divorce, who, after giving their relationship the attention it needed, fell back in love again; every week I receive letters from couples I've never even met, but who share this same kind of success story with me. So it's not just possible—it's happening all the time, and I pray it can happen for you too.

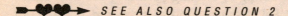 **SEE ALSO QUESTION 2**

8 How can I get my husband to pay as much attention to me as he does to our children?

I consider myself lucky to have a husband who is my best friend, and two healthy young daughters. So I feel even more guilty to admit that I'm jealous of my girls! The truth is, my husband gives them more attention and affection than he gives me. I always brag about what a great dad he is, but I need more physical and emotional closeness with him. I've tried to talk about this, but he ends up feeling criticized and pulls even farther away. Am I expecting too much?

➤━♥♥♥━➤ Guess what? Millions of wives and mothers feel the same secret envy you do about how much love their husband shows the kids, so be assured that you're not "bad," "selfish," or "weird"— you're just not getting everything you need from your partner. (I hear this same complaint from men, too, by the way, about their wife showing the kids more affection.) So the first step is to stop making yourself wrong for longing to be the recipient of the tenderness and caring your husband showers on your daughters. Of course you're jealous: the little girl inside of you is hungry for the intimacy you know your mate is capable of, since you see him share this with your girls. I know it feels awful to see your own daughters, whom you adore, as rivals, but that's what's happening.

It might help you to understand where your

husband is coming from. You see, it's easy for him to be so emotionally generous with his children. *They don't nag him, criticize what he says or does, or see his faults!! In other words, they still love him unconditionally.* That feeling of being loved purely and completely allows him to feel safe enough to open his heart and share the most giving part of himself with them. With you, it's a different story. You don't have him on a pedestal, like the girls do; you don't think everything he says is so smart; you see him as he really is. So it's much more difficult for your husband to feel as safe and loved with you as he does with his daughters. This is true for all parents—it's a lot more challenging to be as consistently loving with our mates as we are with our kids, but that's the whole point of marriage—ideally, to learn how to love another person in spite of their imperfections.

That's the compassionate part of the answer, but the second part is more practical: **Your relationship with your husband must be placed first, before your relationship as parents to the kids.** *I believe strongly that, as a wife, you need to feel you are Number One to your husband, and not that you get the emotional leftovers, if there are any, after your daughters are loved.* If your marriage isn't healthy, it won't matter how much your children feel loved . . . you will end up feeling resentment toward them, and they will not grow up with a positive example of how a woman should be treated. The stronger your relationship with your husband is, the better both of you will be as parents to your kids. Keeping you happy and well loved should be your husband's first responsibility to the family, because that ensures a stable and lasting home life for your children. And the happier you and he are together, the happier your girls will be. Tell him I said so!!!!

9 *How should you handle a partner who smothers you with too much love and affection and is too possessive?*

I have the opposite problem than most women have—my boyfriend loves me too much. He wants to be with me every second; he never takes his hands off me; and when we aren't together, he calls me every few hours. I've asked him to back off, to give me some space, but he gets really hurt and rejected, and I end up comforting him. I really care about this man, but I'm starting to turn off, and even feel scared of him. How can I make him see that I need him to love me less?

➤ ❤❤❤ ➤ Your problem isn't that your boyfriend loves you too much—*it's that he doesn't love himself enough. He's what I call an "emotional vampire."* His heart is like an emotional container that's empty, and he desperately needs you to fill him up, only there's a hole in the bottom, so no matter how much you give him, it will never be enough, and he'll always crave more. No wonder you feel uncomfortable: although he appears to be *giving* in his desire to be with you, touch you, and call you, he's actually *taking*. He's feeding off your attention, your presence, your energy.

People like your boyfriend who seem to "love too much" are almost always desperately needy, seeking to distract themselves from their pain with a temporary dose of love, sex, or affection. They can fall in love instantly, and become easily compulsive and obsessed, sucking their partners in by sweeping them off their feet, and, eventually, keeping them around with guilt and pity. Your boyfriend probably has been very hurt in his life, perhaps by a family member, and he has an emotional wound that will not heal until he deals with it at its source. Your relationship and all the others he has had are like Band-Aids, temporary solutions for a deep and chronic problem.

What am I telling you? Probably to end this relationship now, before things get worse, and they inevitably will. The *only* circumstances under which you should keep seeing him would be if he admitted to the problem and sought help immediately. There's a chance that, if your boyfriend receives some intensive counseling, you could work things out together. However, I sense that you've already had enough. And don't forget to take a look at why you got sucked in by this kind of person. (Hint: He begs for your love—you withhold it . . . Are you punishing Mom or Dad? Are you staying in control?)

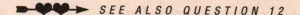 *SEE ALSO QUESTION 12*

10 *How can a couple learn to trust love when they've both been badly hurt in past relationships?*

After surviving a very bitter divorce and custody battle for my children, I finally met a wonderful man who is everything my ex-husband wasn't. He's kind, open, and willing to talk about everything. Our problem is that his ex-wife left him for his best friend, so he's afraid to trust love again, and so am I. How can we leave the past behind us and make this new relationship work?

➡️💗💗➡️ First of all, congratulations!! You are faced with what I call a "high-class problem," a problem that looks like a problem, but is really a great situation with some challenges attached to it. In essence, what you're asking is, "How can my partner and I get rid of the fear in our relationship so we can love fully?" That's a wonderful question to be able to ask. So the first step is for you and your sweetie to remind yourselves that you've worked very hard to get to this place. Before you get too intense about climbing your next mountain, take a moment to stop and really celebrate how far you've both come to finally have found a healthy relationship.

Okay, now, back to the fear. I'm going to say something that might sound strange—*a little fear isn't such a bad thing for you and your boyfriend to feel . . . it will keep you on your toes and force you to pay attention.* I'll bet if you and he look back on your failed marriages, you will notice that you didn't pay attention to warning signs, problems, conflicts, unmet needs, and all kinds of stuff. Eventually, it was precisely what you weren't paying attention to that sabotaged your relationships, right? You didn't treat those relationships carefully enough. So here you are with a new, wonderful partner, and you're both scared of making mistakes again, and a little reluctant to just blindly trust. I say, that's great! It's about time! You *should* be afraid of making mistakes, all of us should. You *should* be careful to make sure your needs get met. *You should be paying very close attention, because the more you pay attention to your relationship, the better it will be.*

Do you get my point? It's like someone who carelessly used a sharp knife and cut herself badly. The next time you pick up the knife to use it, you are afraid. You respect its power much more, as well you should. A relationship is like that—a powerful tool that can be used to help us or hurt us, and I feel not enough people respect that tool.

Here's something practical you can do to help. Each of you should make a *Relationship Mistake List*. Go back and honestly assess your former relationship from the very beginning to the end. Write down every mistake *you* made. Examples: "Let my ex-husband talk me out of my feelings, and then pushed down my resentment." "Didn't ask for what I wanted in bed, and felt dissatisfied." Don't be surprised at how long these lists are. Share yours with your partner, and have him share his. Talk about each item. Then, together, come up with a new *Relationship Rule* for each old mistake, and write these down. Example: "When I disagree with something my partner does or says, I will express my feelings, even if it causes tension between us," or "I will let my partner know what I enjoy sexually so he doesn't have to guess."

The point of this exercise is twofold: First, it will help you understand that your prior relationships didn't just go bad. There were specific unhealthy behaviors and love habits that caused the relationships to fail. *Second, by paying attention to these unhealthy love habits, and committing on paper to new, healthy behavioral choices, you have a great chance of avoiding the old mistakes that would hurt you again.* Throw in some good books, tapes, or seminars on making relationships work, and you will have a great foundation to go forward into this new romance with excitement, enthusiasm, and high hopes.

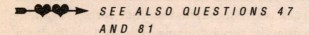

SEE ALSO QUESTIONS 47 AND 81

11 *What does it mean when your partner won't introduce you to his family and friends?*

I've been dating a man for nine months who won't introduce me to his family or his friends. I know he has children from a former marriage, and I haven't even met them. Most of the time, we spend alone at my apartment or his condo, and when we do go out, it's always at the last minute. He claims that he is a private person, and that he doesn't want to bring other people into our relationship, but something doesn't feel right to me. What does this mean?

━━♥♥♥━━ I hate to be the one to tell you this, but this behavior means just what you secretly suspect it means—that your boyfriend is ashamed to be seen with you or associated with you, and is hiding you from the people in his life. It could be that, for some reason, he doesn't think you're "good enough" to be an *official* girlfriend—maybe you don't look the way he thinks you should or come from a background he thinks is acceptable. This may sound terrible, but it's nothing compared to the second possibility you need to look at: *Your boyfriend may be married or involved with someone else, and is cheating on her with you!* Thus, the sneaking around, staying inside, and keeping you isolated from the rest of his life. The signs all add up, don't they?

I'll bet you've known this deep inside yourself, but haven't wanted to face it, because it means confronting him and, if you have any self-respect, ending the relationship immediately. And respect is the key word here. *He obviously doesn't respect you—his behavior is totally disrespectful.* So once you've broken up with him, you need to ask yourself some difficult and confrontational questions: *Why did I put up with this kind of treatment for so long? What in my emotional past attracts me to men who treat me like I'm not important? What are some of the ways I kept myself in denial about something so obvious? How can I begin to heal my own emotional wounds so I don't get hurt like this again?*

It's time for you to love yourself enough to know you don't deserve to be treated like some awful secret too grotesque for the world to see. The man who is lucky enough to be with you should be proud and honored to have you in his life, and excited about showing you off to everyone he knows. And the sooner you get rid of this character you're with, the sooner you'll meet a partner who will treat you like the wonderful human being you are.

12 *How do you heal old emotional hurts from the past so you can have a healthy relationship with your partner?*

Even though I know that many of the problems in my relationship are caused or aggravated by some past hurts from my childhood and from painful love affairs, I still can't figure out how to let go of the past. My husband has his own issues, and between the two of us, I wonder how we've survived this long! Is there a way to heal the past so it doesn't sabotage our relationship?

➤♥♥♥➤ This is one of the most important questions any of us can ask ourselves: *How can I identify and heal any unhealthy emotional patterns formed in my past so they don't sabotage my adult relationships?* In fact, you've just taken the first step in healing yourself: acknowledging the existence of your emotional baggage and expressing a willingness to get rid of it! Sadly, most people in the world will never even admit that their past experiences are emotionally handicapping them in their present lives, and therefore will never have the opportunity to experience what I call "true emotional freedom." *I define emotional freedom as the freedom to live as the person you want to be, and love as much as you want to love. It's freedom from the past to be all you can in the present.*

In order to heal the past, you have to understand what I call your "emotional programming." *Your emotional programming is simply a set of decisions you made about yourself, others, and the world in general when you were growing up.* As an infant, you came into the world like a blank slate. Even though you were born with a certain set of genetic predispositions, you had no experiences yet to affect you either negatively or positively. But each day that you are alive, you collect experiences, and each one teaches you something about yourself and other people. You are either treated well, or treated harshly; you are either loved or neglected; you are either praised or put down.

Each of these experiences helps you form a **decision** about yourself, about people, and about life. For instance, if your parents had an unhappy, turbulent relationship, and as an infant or small child you heard constant fighting, you might have unconsciously decided: "I have to always be good, so I don't make people I love unhappy," or "It's not safe for me to express angry feelings." Here's another example. Let's say your father was emotionally distant and not there for you. You may have unconsciously decided "I can't count on the people I love," or "People who love me abandon me." Each experience you have as a child helps you make certain decisions, until you have a collection of decisions you have made about life. **This collection of decisions or beliefs is called your emotional programming.** In the same way you would program a computer with basic information, and the computer would use that information to do tasks or solve problems, so you program your mind with this emotional programming. For the rest of your life, this "program" affects how you think, how you behave, and especially, how you react to circumstances that remind you of your painful childhood experiences.

The majority of this emotional programming occurs when you are still very young. Psychologists estimate that:

Between the ages of 0–5 years old	You receive 50% of your emotional programming
Between the ages of 5–8 years old	You receive 30% of your emotional programming

That means, by the age of 8 you are 80% programmed psychologically. In other words, 80% of the decisions about yourself and others have already been made.

Between the ages of 8–18 years old	You receive 15% more of your emotional programming

So by the time you are eighteen years old, you're 95 percent complete! That leaves 5 percent for the rest of your life. This may not seem like much, but it's that 5 percent that I work with when I help people make changes in their lives. And the good news is that you can use that 5 percent to understand and change the other 95 percent!

Perhaps now you can better understand why it's easy to be so unaware of what motivates you in your relationships. The 5 percent of your mind that is conscious says "I want to be a loving husband to my wife" but the 95 percent of your mind that is *unconscious* may be programmed to avoid intimacy and keep a wall around your heart.

In my Making Love Work at-home video and audio seminar, I talk about a three-step healing process that you can use to eliminate your emotional programming:

1. *Identify, feel, and express the old, unresolved emotions that are trapped inside your heart so that you can "Work them out, not act them out."*

2. *Understand your old, unhealthy love choices, and then make new, healthy love choices which will heal your old fear and build new trust.*

3. *Open up to new, positive experiences of love that will heal the old pain which was caused by some lack of love.*

I strongly suggest that you find a system of emotional healing that incorporates both experiential work in releasing old emotions and practical, action-oriented behavioral changes to build healthy new habits.

Now I'll bet you're thinking, "Boy, this sounds like a lot of work." And it can be. But the rewards are worth it—the freedom to give and receive the kind of love you've always wanted!

13 *How important is sexual chemistry in a relationship? If it's not there in the beginning, will it develop over time?*

━♥♥➤ People who ask me this question are usually involved in a relationship they wish were different. They feel love for their partner, but don't feel sexually attracted to them. *They don't want to leave, so they try to rationalize their lack of sexual chemistry and make it "okay."*

My honest response to this question is:

"NO, I DON'T BELIEVE IT IS POSSIBLE TO HAVE A HEALTHY, LASTING, ROMANTIC RELATIONSHIP WITH SOMEONE WHOM YOU AREN'T ATTRACTED TO, *at least for me or anyone else who wants to include sexuality as a part of our lives."* After all, it is sex that distinguishes an intimate relationship from a friendship. Perhaps if a couple met when they were both quite elderly and no longer had an interest in sex, they wouldn't need more than a strong friendship as a foundation to live together happily. But there is no reason people in their seventies and even older can't enjoy active and fulfilling sex lives, so I don't even like to use this example. Besides, it's not sixty- or seventy-year-olds who usually ask me about love without attraction— it's men and women in their twenties, thirties, and forties.

If you're not attracted to a partner, can the sexual chemistry develop over time? That depends. For instance, if you have an issue like the woman in Question 15, where she isn't normally sexually attracted to nice guys, you could develop sexual attraction over time by doing some emotional healing. *However, if this pattern or any kind of sexual dysfunction or abuse hasn't been a problem for you, and you simply haven't felt sexually attracted to your partner from the beginning of your relationship, you'll be unlikely to develop it over time.*

If you're in a relationship with someone you've never been sexually attracted to, here are some things to think about:

1. ***You are avoiding true intimacy.*** A sexual connection binds a couple together in a very special way. *There is nothing more intimate than taking someone inside your own body, if you are a woman, or putting a part of yourself into someone else, if you are a man.* Especially when you are making love, and not just having sex, you create tremendous intimacy between yourself and your partner. **Although it may look like you are avoiding sex, becoming involved with someone to whom you aren't attracted may actually be a way you are unconsciously avoiding intimacy in your life.** Since you know you aren't going to have a strong sexual relationship, you are naturally protected from feeling too vulnerable with your partner.

2. *You are avoiding sex.* Some people aren't just avoiding intimacy by selecting mates they aren't attracted to—they are avoiding sex. If . . .

- You have experienced any form of sexual molestation or abuse
- You have been raped
- You have felt sexually controlled by previous partners
- You were brought up with negative sexual programming

. . . then you may unconsciously fall in love with people who don't turn you on sexually. This way you get to avoid sex. You may not be aware that you have these sexual issues. You may even bemoan the fact that you keep attracting partners in whom you're not sexually interested. *But if lack of chemistry is a recurring theme in your relationships, you may need to do some work on healing your sexuality.*

3. *You are trying to maintain a position of control.* When you feel sexually attracted to someone, you are, in a sense, giving them some control over you. It's as if your mind is saying "You affect me so strongly that you make me want to lose control around you." *If you have issues* *with needing to be in control, or being afraid of being controlled by others, you may choose partners toward whom you feel no or little sexual attraction in order to keep yourself "safe."* Because you don't feel a strong sexual pull toward them, you get to maintain a certain emotional distance, creating the illusion that you hold more of the power in the relationship.

This is one of the most difficult, yet most important issues a couple should face before getting seriously involved. As painful as it may be, think carefully about everything I've said, and make your decision based on what you know in your heart to be true.

14 How do you motivate someone to want to change and open up emotionally?

Every time I try to talk to my husband about working on our relationship, he says he's "happy with the way things are." I'm not happy, but no matter what I do, he shows no interest in changing or growing. How can I motivate him to want to open up more?

➤━❤❤❤━➤ I'm going to give you an answer you don't want to hear: *You can't motivate another person to grow and change. He has to motivate himself.* That may sound logical, but I know how painful it is to accept when you really love someone, and know that if he doesn't open up and grow, your relationship probably won't make it. In my own life, I've faced this same dilemma several times, and understand how much it hurts to see your partner resisting the very kinds of help that would ultimately save your marriage. It's like watching someone you love drowning in the ocean, and wanting to save him, but when you throw him a life preserver, he pushes it away, claiming he doesn't need it. You know that if he doesn't reach out, you will lose him, so you plead with him to grab hold. Stubbornly, he refuses, and you are forced to see him slip away.

Here's one of the most important lessons I've ever learned about love: *Some people just aren't capable of loving you the way you want to be loved, or capable of having the kind of relationship you need.* It's not that they are trying to be difficult, or stubborn, or deliberately trying to make you unhappy. They simply cannot operate on the same emotional level you operate on, nor do they want to. Unfortunately, most couples don't discuss these issues sufficiently in the beginning of the relationship so they can determine whether they have enough emotional compatibility to live happily together. They fall in love, have a family, and then realize they are two very different people with very conflicting pictures of what they want and need from an intimate relationship. One partner isn't right, and the other wrong—the problem is that their love styles are incompatible.

This is what I suggest: Without blaming him, and without making him feel like the bad guy, sit down with your husband and share something like the following . . . *"I love you very much, and have tried for 'X' years to make this relationship work. I know you're aware that I've been begging you to open up, to work on our marriage, to talk about issues we have. I've been doing this for one reason—to try and save our marriage, because I'm not happy with the way things are. You've always told me you're satisfied with this kind of relationship, that you aren't interested in growing or changing in the way I am, and I haven't respected what you've said, and have tried to get you to change. Now I realize that I was wrong in doing this. You have the right to live just the way you want to, and so do I. My way isn't better than yours—it's just different.*

"So, honey, I need you to take as much time as you need, days or a few weeks, to ask yourself one last time if you are happy living as the person you are, and do not want a relationship where your partner needs you to open up or work on yourself. If you come to me and tell me this is definitely how you feel, then I will know it's time for me to go on without you. See, I do want a relationship in which I and my partner are always growing and changing together, and actively working on becoming more intimate and more loving. That is one of the most important things in my life. I would love to have that kind of marriage with you, but if that's not what you want, I will understand, and free myself to one day find someone who shares my vision of love, and free you to find someone who loves you just the way you are."

Find the emotional courage to have this conversation with your husband. It will be one of the most difficult yet loving things you've ever done, not just for you, but for him. I've had people tell me that, after hearing it put this way, their partner miraculously went through a total change and dedicated himself or herself to tremendous personal growth, so it's possible. Whatever the outcome, know that it's time to turn the corner in your life, one way or the other, and experience the kind of relationship you've always dreamed of.

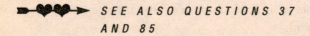 SEE ALSO QUESTIONS 37 AND 85

Compatibility

15
Why am I only attracted to the wrong, "bad boy" type of man, and feel no sexual chemistry with the "nice guys"?

For years I have had a series of very painful, dramatic relationships with men who don't give me what I need or treat me the way I deserve to be treated. Some cheated, others were very critical, or simply emotionally distant. Finally, I met a really nice guy who is crazy about me. He's everything I ever wanted—respectful, considerate, and really sweet. But there's one big thing missing: I don't feel the sexual chemistry with him that I used to feel with my ex-boyfriends. Lately I've been feeling I should break up with him, because I miss that passion and excitement. Help!!

━❤❤❤━ You've come to the right place for help—not only is this one of the questions I'm asked most often, but I used to suffer from this same pattern and wonder what was wrong with me. Why did men who didn't love me the way I wanted to be loved appeal to me so much? Why did I get "bored" in calm, peaceful relationships? Why did the phrase "nice guy" turn off every sexual impulse in my body? It took me years to understand and finally break this unhealthy love habit, but I did it, so I know you can do it too.

Okay, here's what's happening. You've obviously already figured out that it's no accident that you happen to attract (or be attracted to) men who, in some way, make you feel unloved, and you're right

. . . there's a reason it feels "right" when you're with a man who withholds his love, and a reason it feels "wrong" when a man gives you all the love you've ever wanted. This reason has nothing to do with what your conscious mind tells you about those unloving partners: *"You know he is wrong for you. He's just going to hurt you like the last one. Run in the other direction as fast as you can!!"* You may know this is true, but something makes that kind of man so appealing, and that something has to do with your unconscious mind and what I call the "Going Home Syndrome."

I came up with the phrase "Going Home Syndrome" to describe how our emotional programming (see Question 12) can *cause us to seek out emotional situations that are similar to those we experienced in childhood, regardless of whether those experiences were positive or negative.* As human beings, we gravitate toward the familiar. I'll bet you like to sleep on the same side of the bed each night, park in the same space at work, and go back to your favorite vacation spot. *Returning to the familiar* is a basic instinct that gives our lives a sense of continuity and safety in a very chaotic and changing universe. Unfortunately, this instinct can work against us when it comes to relationships, in that we may tend to unconsciously seek out emotional situations that are familiar to us.

Here's how it works: When you were a young

child, your home was the main source of love and safety in your life. Even if there was violence or chaos in your household, it was still "home"—it was where you were fed and had a place to sleep and received some sort of attention. So you associate LOVE with HOME. You also associate HOME with other characteristics, based on your experiences at home. For instance, if your parents fought a lot, you might have an equation in your mind that says **HOME = CHAOS.** If you weren't shown much love or affection your equation might be **HOME = LONELINESS.** If one of your parents was abusive, it might be **HOME = FEAR.**

Remember your basic math from school, where you learned:

If A = B, and B = C, then A = C

Let's use this same principle to illustrate "Going Home":

If LOVE = HOME, and HOME = CHAOS, then **LOVE = CHAOS**

If LOVE = HOME, and HOME = LONELINESS, then **LOVE = LONELINESS**

If LOVE = HOME, and HOME = FEAR, then **LOVE = FEAR.**

Your mind will equate whatever associations you have about "home" with what love is supposed to feel like. So if home felt like chaos, you might seek unstable partners who will help you create dramatic, chaotic relationships. If home felt like loneliness, you might seek a partner who doesn't give you enough love, affection, or attention, so that you end up feeling lonely. If home felt like fear, you might attract someone who always criticizes you, or threatens to leave, or makes you jealous, so that you always feel fearful. You unconsciously choose what is familiar—**YOU ARE GOING HOME.**

Obviously, we all have positive associations with home as well, which we also seek to reproduce in our adult life. I've found, however, that *it is the more painful associations that can cause the most trouble, because they are usually unconscious.* In other words, if you came from a home where your parents showed you a lot of affection, but criticized one another, you might consciously seek a partner who was very loving, but unconsciously attract someone who was critical.

In your case, your previous partners were probably all "home" to you, possibly because when you grew up, you either watched your mom or dad be mistreated and abandoned by the other parent, or you felt unloved by one of your parents. So for you, it feels comfortable to be uncomfortable with a man! And this explains your present dilemma. *You have love, and therefore passion and sexual attraction, associated in your brain with a sense of danger and pain. Of course you don't "feel" attracted to your "nice guy"—he makes you feel too good!!*

As I mentioned, I had a very similar pattern for years of my adult life. When I finally met my husband, Jeffrey, I didn't even realize I was in love for months, because it didn't "feel right." I was used to drama, intensity, fear of criticism and loss, insecurity—all signs of an unhealthy relationship. For the first time, I had developed an emotional connection with a man based on friendship, trust, openness, safety, consistency, and true caring, and I hadn't even recognized it **because it felt too peaceful to be love!!**

It took a little while for me to discover the healthy passion and excitement with Jeffrey, and to literally reinvent my experience of love, but when I finally did, I felt more attracted to him than I had felt to any other man in my life!! So my advice to you is: Don't break up with this wonderful man. He's the best thing that ever happened to you. Instead, do some work to explore and heal your emotional programming: LEAVE BEHIND THE PATTERN, NOT THE PERSON!!

SEE ALSO QUESTIONS 12 AND 25

16 *Can a relationship work when you're in love with your partner's potential?*

A few months ago I met a man I really care about. We get along well, but he's going through a difficult time right now. He's just recovering from a serious drug addiction and a bad divorce in which his ex-wife got most of his savings. I know he has a lot of anger and mistrust from his past, and he has a hard time showing any affection, but inside, he's a very sensitive, talented person, and I feel like he needs someone to believe in him. Can this relationship work?

➤❤❤❤➤ I wouldn't call what you're in a relationship—it's closer to gambling, and I'm sorry to say the odds are against you. *You aren't in love with who your boyfriend actually is; you're in love with who you hope he could become. You even talk about him like he is a project, a "fixer-upper."* You're describing someone who is barely capable of loving himself right now, let alone you. Obviously, every relationship between two people involves some hopes and dreams of how you'd like to see your partner grow and improve. But the key is feeling satisfied with how your mate is today, not living for the future. **Having a healthy relationship with a person means loving him for who he is now, not loving him in spite of his situation, or in hope of who he will change into tomorrow.**

Inside, you know all this, yet you ignore the facts because something about this situation is so appealing to you, almost irresistible, and very hard to walk away from. That's what we need to talk about. People who fall in love with their partner's potential tend to have several issues of their own that attract them to this kind of situation:

1) *You need to be in control in relationships.* When you love someone in order to improve him, you get to feel superior. Perhaps you felt controlled or criticized for never being good enough as a child, and now you unconsciously are attracted to someone whom you can turn the tables on.

2) *You get to avoid your own life and dreams by focusing on rehabilitating your partner.* When you're busy looking at how someone else can improve, you don't have much time left over to face your own sense of inadequacy or your own fears.

3) *You made a decision as a child that you couldn't get what you wanted.* If you felt rejected or unloved as a child, you may have decided you can't get what you want from people you love, and so you unconsciously seek out a man who doesn't give you what you want. You're "going home" (see Question 15).

If you care about this man, end the relationship now. Does that sound strange? Well, here's what will happen if you don't. Soon you will end up feeling angry at him for letting you down, bitter that you wasted so much time with him, and guilty for rejecting him after you promised undying love and patience. Ending it now will free him to do the healing he needs, and will open you up to attracting someone you can love and respect as he is *today*.

Is there such a thing as being too "picky" when choosing partners?

I'm single, in my thirties, and having a hard time finding the right person to spend my life with. All of my friends accuse me of being too picky, and warn me that I'll never find anyone if I don't compromise more. I'm afraid if I'm less careful, I'll end up settling for someone who isn't right for me. What's the answer?

➡❤❤➤ Here's what "too picky" means: You meet a potential mate who has all of the qualities you've been looking for . . . except you love tennis and he doesn't, so you disqualify him immediately; or you get to know someone who seems to be just what you've always wanted . . . except she could lose about ten pounds, so you end the relationship. See what I mean? A person is too picky when he finds small things about a potential partner that probably won't affect the core of the relationship, and uses those missing items as excuses to avoid intimacy and cover up his fear of not being good enough himself— *"I'll reject you before you have a chance to reject me."* So perhaps this describes you, and if it does, take a look at the fear that underlies your hypercritical attitude.

I have a sense, however, that in your case, *you are simply being choosy, not picky.* You are holding out for the kind of person you truly want to spend the rest of your life with, one with whom you are highly compatible in all the important areas of your life. I talk about ten areas of compatibility that you should look for in a mate:

1) *Physical style:* appearance, personal fitness, and eating habits, etc.

2) *Emotional style:* attitude toward relationships and affection, ability to express feelings

3) *Social style:* personality traits, how he interacts with others

4) *Intellectual style:* educational background, attitude toward learning, creative expressions, cultural experience

5) *Sexual style:* sexual experience and skill, ability to enjoy sex, attitude

6) *Communication style:* how he communicates, attitude toward communication

7) *Professional/Financial style:* relationship with money, attitude toward success, work and organizational habits

8) *Personal Growth style:* attitude toward self-improvement, willingness to work on relationship, ability to change self

9) *Spiritual style:* attitude toward Higher Power, spiritual practices, philosophy of life, moral views

10) *Hobbies and interests*

You don't have to have total compatibility in all these areas, but in the ones that are most important to you, you should have very strong compatibility. (For an extensive discussion of compatibility and how to determine it, pick up my book *"Are You the One for Me?"*)

The truth is, I wish more people were as "choosy" as you. There would be fewer divorces and dysfunctional relationships. So don't let yourself be pressured by your family or friends to compromise what you know in your heart is important. And don't give in to the artificially manufactured social time-clock that says you "must" be married before a certain age. Remember, your soul mate is waiting for you out there. He (or she) doesn't want you to give up looking before you find him. "Hang in there!" he's whispering. And when you find him, I know it will have been worth the wait, and you won't care how long it took.

➤♥♥➤ *SEE ALSO QUESTION 26*

Last year I met a wonderful man at a friend's wedding, and we've been having a relationship ever since. The problem is that we live in two different parts of the country, two thousand miles away from each other. Does our relationship have a chance? How can we keep it working when we are so far apart?

━━♥♥➤ Of course your relationship has a chance, but since it is a long-distance romance, you have to be aware of the possible problems and do what you can to avoid them. The very same factors that make a long-distance relationship so exciting also make it hazardous. *It's easy for you to think the relationship is much better than it is because you don't spend consistent quality time together.* Your goal becomes trying to see one another again, rather than really taking a close look at the relationship.

There are three major problems in long-distance relationships:

1) *You don't get to see what your partner is really like.*

> You know that if you have three days to spend with your lover, you are going to be on your best behavior and so is he. It's easy to hide the difficult parts of your personality for seventy-two hours, and leave feeling won-

derful. But you never really get to know one another, because you don't see your mate under pressure, in a crisis, when he is ill, when he is frightened. All of these situations reveal a lot about someone's character, an essential part of determining compatibility. You need consistent time to discover these dimensions of a person.

2) *You avoid dealing with problem areas.*

Let's imagine that you haven't seen your long-distance lover in two months, and he's flown in to spend the weekend with you. Over dinner that night, he says something that annoys you. Now you have to make a decision: Do you confront him on what is upsetting you, and risk ruining your weekend, or do you forget about it? Most people choose to avoid the confrontation, fearful that by the time they get through the argument and hurt feelings, half of the weekend will already be over. *The problem with this habit is that you and your partner never learn to problem solve together, or advance the relationship to deeper levels of communication and harmony. The unresolved issues and the unexpressed resentments just sit there like Emotional Time Bombs, waiting to explode.* It may look like you have a great relationship on the surface, but you haven't allowed it to move through the transition stage every healthy love affair must experience.

3) *You have an unrealistic view of your compatibility.*
Long-distance lovers often don't even know how little they have in common because they are too busy entertaining themselves. *If you only have three days with your partner, you will treat it like a mini-vacation*—you'll spend all your time together; you'll go out to restaurants, movies, shows, etc.; you'll have lots of sex; and you'll avoid friends and family. This gives you a very unrealistic picture of your relationship. You may actually enjoy the excitement of the fun weekend more than you enjoy your partner and not even know it. Many couples find themselves extremely disappointed when they finally move to the same city or decide to live together. *"It doesn't feel like it used to,"* they often complain. Of course it doesn't. *It's not a twenty-four-hour-a-day party anymore. It's a real full-time relationship, and if you and your partner aren't truly compatible, you'll find out real fast.*

For a long-distance romance to evolve into a healthy, lasting relationship, *both partners will eventually have to live in the same place.* That's the only way you can truly know if you are compatible, and develop the level of intimacy you need to sustain your love. *But while you're still apart, the most successful long-distance affairs are those in which the couple treats the relationship like it is a full-time romance. So:*

- Don't try to make every moment together special, but do normal things together
- Don't try to hide difficult parts of your personalities, but be yourselves
- Don't edit how you feel, but allow yourselves to communicate honestly and deal with conflicts as they come up.

How important are cultural differences in a relationship?

My fiancée and I are from very different cultural back-grounds—hers is much more traditional and strict, socially and spiritually, than mine as an American. We've always told ourselves that our love was more important than where we were born, but we're starting to run into some very big problems as we discuss wedding plans, having children, and other serious issues. Am I making a mistake in telling myself the differences don't matter?

➤ Don't kid yourself . . . differences *always* matter—it's just a question of how many there are and how much conflict they create in the relationship. *Love is not enough to make a relationship work: you need compatibility,* and as you're discovering, cultural differences aren't just about where you were born. They spill over into most areas of your life, from your spiritual beliefs; your social, intellectual, and emotional style; your values; your choices about child-rearing; customs; and on and on. It's not that you and your partner have to agree on everything and have gone through the same life experiences. *But there's a point beyond which too many differences will create too much tension, and make a harmonious relationship next to impossible.*

You're experiencing what many engaged couples go through—you're just now confronting some big issues between you that hadn't fully surfaced before. I'll bet you both avoided seriously talking about some of the cultural differences while you were dating because, intuitively, you knew they would be "hot buttons." So here you are engaged and Pandora's box is opening!! And I can hear that you're having some serious doubts. *That's what an engagement is supposed to be for—a period of time during which you can really take an honest look at all of your remaining issues, and hopefully, come to agreement on how you will blend both of your cultural backgrounds together.*

I know what's scaring you . . . it's possible that as you confront these topics you may discover that your values and beliefs are just too different for you to live compatibly together. As uncomfortable as it will be, find the courage to talk about everything that's bothering you. After all, if it's not going to work, isn't it better to find out now, rather than waiting until after you are married and have children?

20 Is it damaging to a relationship when one partner is still controlled by his parents?

My fiancé is thirty-three, but he might as well be three years old, because his parents still control him, especially his mother. He talks to her on the phone every single day, and she calls here at all hours, with no respect for our schedule. Now that we're engaged, she is pushing all of her ideas about the wedding on him, and we end up fighting about her constantly. I've tried to get him to look at his relationship with both of his parents, but he says they're just a close family, and that there's nothing abnormal about it. My childhood was very unhappy, and I have a very distant relationship with my own parents, so I wonder if I'm judging him unfairly. Help!

➤❤❤❤➤ Why are you asking me this question? You already know the answer. *You can't marry someone who is emotionally married to one or both of his parents. You can't marry someone who hasn't grown up.* Well, actually, you can marry someone like that, but you'll be miserable. You have every classic sign of coming face to face with what I call *"Toxic In-Laws."* Toxic in-laws do not respect the boundaries of your relationship and the boundaries between them and your spouse. They will interfere in your life, become time and energy vampires, and even refuse to acknowledge you or your relationship, because to them, you are an outsider. They haven't let go of their son and will resent you for taking him away from them.

Do these things sound bad? Well, they're nothing compared to how *toxic in-laws will drive a wedge between you and your partner by creating dissension in your relationship*. It sounds like that's already happening with you and your fiancé. You end up feeling unsupported and misunderstood by him, furious at his parents for manipulating him, and everyone starts thinking you're a real bitch! And if you think it's bad now, wait until you have children!!

In spite of what you may believe, your fiancé's parents aren't the problem—he is. If he took a stand with his parents and set boundaries in their relationship, it wouldn't make any difference how much they tried to interfere. He needs to make you number one in his life. You need to be his first priority; your marriage has to come first before his relationship with his mother and father.

The children of toxic in-laws need to communicate the following information to their parents if they want to save their relationships with their partners:

1. *I have chosen my spouse to be my lifelong mate, and I expect you to treat her (him) with total respect, courtesy, and warmth. We are a couple, and when you criticize or hurt my partner, it is the same as hurting me.*

2. *If you cannot bring yourself to behave with respect around my spouse, then I do not wish*

to see you. You will either see us together and treat us with love, or not see us at all.

3. *My home is mine, not yours. When you come over, you will call first, and if we want to see you, we will tell you. When you do come over you will not tell me or my wife how to run our lives, raise our children, arrange our furniture, etc.*

4. *You need to respect our time and privacy. That means I do not wish you to call my house five times a day. Give us the space to want to call you. Naturally I will be here for you if there is a real emergency.*

5. *I know this may be difficult for you to understand, but that's the way it is. I want you in my life, but not if you cannot accept my marriage and respect our relationship.*

If you discuss this with your partner, and he repeatedly refuses to confront his parents, you can try suggesting counseling so he can get a third opinion. If he refuses that, you need to ask yourself why you are staying in this relationship. It isn't going to get any better, and you know it's already tearing you apart. Do not get married unless this is resolved!!

21 *Why do I always fall in love with people who need rescuing?*

I'm presently dating a woman who's basically a mess. She has major financial and emotional problems, and I spend a lot of my time playing "Daddy," trying to help her. I can't believe I'm in this kind of relationship again—it's the third time in a row I've gotten involved with "victim-type" women. Why am I doing this, and how do I stop?

➤ ❤❤❤ ➤ Why are you doing this? Because you *like* rescuing women . . . you like feeling strong, important, superior . . . you like being in control. Rescueholics are drawn to wounded, fragile, unloved partners like flies to honey. These relationships suck you in, and once you're in, boy is it hard to get out!! The good news is that you've finally recognized the pattern, and sound desperate enough to change it.

Remember—in all codependent relationships, the rescuer needs the victim as much as the victim needs the rescuer. If you are an "emotional Robin Hood," always finding partners in need of your help, you may in fact be completing unfinished business from childhood, acting out your little boy's unfulfilled need to fix or rescue Mom, Dad, or another family member. Or maybe you're attempting to rescue yourself as you felt when you were small. *The problem is that like all rescuers, you are mistaking sympathy for love.*

You already know from experience that this sort of relationship is doomed. You end up acting like a parent, tiptoeing around your partner in order to not upset her, and making excuses for her behavior. Ultimately, your resentment grows and although you want to leave, you feel trapped, too guilty to leave and hurt even more this poor wounded person you wanted to heal. When you do inevitably leave, you feel like you're abandoning your lover, and beat yourself up for "failing." Sounds like lots of fun. . . .

You asked me how you could stop. My answer: *Just stop.* End this relationship before it gets any worse; encourage your girlfriend to get help dealing with her need to be rescued, and take some time to look at your own issues and needs that have addicted you to this kind of unhealthy love pattern. *Make a list of all the qualities you want in a woman; make a second list of all the warning signs that someone is a potential "victim-type" mate. Read these lists constantly.* Put copies everywhere. When you go out on a date with a new woman, read the lists before, during, and after the date if you have to. This will help you resist the temptation to get involved with another rescue job again while you're healing on the inside.

22 Can a big age difference between two people hurt the relationship?

I'm in love with a great guy who happens to be twenty-two years older than I am—I'm thirty-one and he's fifty-three. He's been married and divorced and has children not much younger than me. My family thinks I'm making a big mistake, and have come right out and told me that they don't approve of the relationship. Am I being naive to think our age differences don't matter?

➤ Yes, you're naive if you think your age differences don't matter. They do, but so do all the other differences in your circumstances and personalities. So ignoring this issue, or any issue, won't work. The more you insist that there aren't any problems, the more you are probably suppressing your concerns for fear that they will sabotage the relationship. Both you and your partner need to honestly and directly face and discuss all the various problems that have or could emerge around your age difference.

Significant age differences between partners can cause serious problems in relationships. *The word "significant" is important here: If your partner is four or five years older or younger, it won't make much of a difference. However, if your partner is ten or more years older or younger than you, it can cause difficulties depending on your ages and other aspects of your personalities.* I've found that age differences mean less as both partners get older. For instance, a fifteen-year age difference between a thirty-five-year-old man and a twenty-year-old woman will probably create more potential hazards than that age span in a sixty-five-year-old man and a fifty-year-old woman. The age difference will affect the first couple more, since their maturity and experience levels are usually much more dissimilar than the second couple's.

Here are the most common issues couples face when there is an age difference:

IF YOU ARE THE OLDER PARTNER:

1. **You can become impatient with your mate.**

   If you are significantly older than your mate, *you may lose patience with her level of immaturity, lack of life experience, and learning process.* This will be especially true if your mate is between twenty and thirty years of age. After all, you've already gone through a lot of what she's dealing with; you've realized it's not the end of the world when you go through a crisis, because it always works out in the end; you've made mistakes and figured out how to do things the right way. So it's not easy watching your younger partner stumble through these same life experiences.

2. **You have a tendency to act like a parent to your mate.**

   When you have ten, twenty, or thirty more years of life experience than your partner has, you will find it next to impossible not to offer advice, correct, and direct him or her. After all, you've been through this before—you know the best way to do it. Of course your intentions are loving; you're only trying to help. But the effect can be very destructive to your relationship. *YOU BEGIN ACTING LIKE A PARENT AND TREATING YOUR PARTNER LIKE A CHILD.* Naturally, your mate feels as if you don't trust her, you don't respect her, and responds just like a rebellious teenager would—she becomes resentful and pulls away. And this parent-child game will quickly destroy the passion in your sex life, since your relationship starts taking on incestuous overtones.

3. **You may be much more financially successful than your partner.**

Most older partners have more financial stability, and therefore more power in the relationship. You've had many more years to build up your income, purchase property and possessions, etc. This financial superiority can create tension between you and your partner in numerous ways—you may feel resentful about being the one who provides more, especially if you are a woman; you may feel like you should make the important decisions

(what to spend, where to live, what kind of
vacation to take) because it's your money, and
your partner might not feel this is fair. You
may have difficulty lowering your standards
of living to accommodate your mate's.

4. **You may be tempted to control your partner
   because you hold more of the power in the
   relationship.**

   All of the warning signs above add up to
   this one—it's easy when you are much older
   than your partner to get into a power trip and
   become controlling. You have more money,
   success, experience and therefore it's tempt-
   ing to "pull rank" on your mate.

5. **You may be tempted to compromise or sacrifice your interests, friends, and activities in
   order to appear more compatible with your
   partner.**

   If your mate is much younger, you may
   give up interests he or she doesn't appreciate
   and take on habits that make you appear
   younger.

If you're involved with a much younger person,
here are some questions to ask yourself:
   "Do I respect my partner?"
   "Am I proud of my partner?"

"Do I trust my partner?"

"What am I learning from my partner?"

IF YOU ARE THE YOUNGER PARTNER:

1. **You may put your partner on a pedestal and give up your power.**

   If your mate is much older than you are, he or she is probably more successful, experienced, and financially secure. This may influence you into unconsciously feeling your partner is "better" than you are, and tempt you to idealize him rather than see him for who he really is. *When you allow yourself to feel lesser because of your mate's chronological advantage, you give up your power. You take his advice rather than trusting your own; you blindly believe his criticisms of you rather than questioning whether or not he's correct; you invalidate your own needs and feelings out of deference to your partner.* You tell yourself:

   "He's the one who's paying for it, so we'll do it his way."

   "I'm sure he knows what he's doing. After all, look how successful he is."

   "He knows much more about these things than I do because he's older."

   Even if your partner doesn't want to play this role with you, you may be tempted to fall into this pattern simply because of the age difference. And if your partner happens to enjoy his role as the older, wiser one, or actually uses it to control you, watch out—your relationship won't be very healthy.

2. **You may set your partner up to be like a parent.**

Another consequence of being the less experienced, less worldly one in a relationship is that you may be tempted to re-create a parent/child dynamic with your partner. *If you are always asking his advice, counting on him to help you, depending on him for money, using his connections to your advantage, allowing him to make decisions for you, you are, in essence, behaving like a child* and giving him the authority to be your father (or if you're the younger man, your mother). This prevents you from truly growing up and opens the door for all kinds of emotional programming to run itself out.

Even when your partner doesn't control you, you may *feel* controlled and intimidated just by virtue of the fact that he or she is that much older. You may react by becoming rebellious, withdrawn, or difficult. Perhaps this is the relationship you had with your own parents, or you may be acting out the anger you never had the courage to express to them when you were growing up.

3. **You may be tempted to compromise or sacrifice your interests, friends, and activities in order to appear more compatible with your partner.**

   If you are involved with a much older person, here are some questions to ask yourself:

   "Does my partner respect me?"
   "Does my partner treat me as an equal?"
   "Do I feel like an equal with my partner?"

In your case, there are two other issues you and your boyfriend *must* discuss: First, whether or not you want children and expect him to start a second family; and how you both plan to deal with your respective families (your parents, his children).

So that's what to watch out for. Now, the good news—a relationship between two people of very different ages *can* work if both partners avoid falling into the patterns we've just talked about by being aware of them, communicating about their feelings, and making agreements that help create an equal and respectful relationship. *The more you have in common and the more committed you are to working on the relationship, the better your chances for survival.*

➡➡➡ SEE ALSO QUESTION 17

23 Can a relationship with an addict (drugs, alcohol, etc.) work?

I love my boyfriend very much, but he has a problem with drugs. I've asked him to stop, even threatened to leave many times, and he always promises he will change, but he never does. I don't want to leave him, but I can't live like this. What should I do?

━♥♥♥➤ You know what you should do. You should leave. When you are involved with a person who has an addiction, you are playing with fire and are sure to get burned. If your partner has an addiction, he is in love with something other than you— the alcohol, the drugs, etc. **He is, in effect, cheating on you.** You are in a love triangle. *That substance is your rival—it will take his time, his attention, and his spirit away from you.* You will end up hating it as much as you would hate another woman, or if you're male, another man.

Here's the second point: *Loving an addict also means loving someone who is a slave*—he is enslaved to drugs, alcohol, sexual addictions, gambling, or some activity that has become his master. He is not a free person. As you've already discovered, you will have a hard time getting an addict to admit he is a slave, because he secretly knows he is controlled by the activity or substance that is his master, and he *will cover up that sense of impotence with denial*. To admit he is addicted would mean admitting he has been powerless, a very frightening and humbling experience, yet crucial in recovery.

The third negative effect addictions have on your relationship is that they interfere with your partner's ability to be intimate with you. Addictive substances used regularly numb one's ability to feel. This habit of emotional numbness will make it difficult for your partner to feel as much as you'd like him to. You will end up feeling very lonely in the relationship.

Relationships are difficult enough without knowingly getting involved with someone still enslaved by an addiction. Does that mean I don't think the addicted person deserves to be loved? Of course not. It means that he or she needs to get into recovery, free himself of the addiction, and understand the pain beneath it before he's capable of having a healthy relationship with anyone. You've tried to get through to your boyfriend before, but try these steps one last time:

1. Tell your partner that you refuse *to live with an addict any longer.*

2. Tell him you will stay with him *only if he agrees to get some help and takes action IMME-DIATELY.*

3. Tell him that if he does not get help immediately, *you are leaving and not coming back.*

4. Stick to your word, and if your partner does not get immediate help, do not give him another chance. *LEAVE*.

5. *DO NOT RETURN unless your partner is clean and sober,* involved in a recovery program, and shows very significant behavioral and attitudinal changes.

6. Take a look at your own codependency by getting involved with Al-Anon, or doing some work on healing your own patterns so you don't attract another addicted personality into your life.

I have a pattern in my relationships that I can't seem to break. I fall in love with people who will not or cannot make a commitment to me. They are either involved with someone else, still recovering from a bad relationship, afraid of commitment, or don't love me enough to want to get really serious. What's wrong with me? Why do I keep choosing people who can't love me?

➤❤❤➤ This is one of the most painful and self-destructive patterns, isn't it? At least you're aware that you are making the choices, and aren't blaming your partners for betraying you. Read the answers to Questions 12 and 15 to learn about emotional programming in general. And remember—nothing is wrong with you that isn't wrong with anyone else. We each have areas of our life where we are the most challenged and carry emotional baggage from our past.

More specifically, you may be prone to choosing unavailable partners if:

- **You felt abandoned by a parent as a child:** You repeat this pattern as an adult by *finding partners who can't be there for you either.*
- **You have low self-esteem:** If you came from a very dysfunctional home which left you with little self-esteem because you were always

criticized or ignored or abused, *you may feel
you don't deserve to have a mate all to yourself, so
you'll take whatever you can get.*

- **You're afraid of intimacy:** Being in a relationship with a partner who is unavailable is a
great way to avoid true intimacy. *If you were
sexually or physically abused as a child and had
your boundaries violated, or made a decision when
you were young that you would never let anyone
get close enough to hurt you again, you may find
it "convenient" to choose partners with whom you
can never have a truly committed relationship as
an unconscious method of protecting yourself from
pain.*

**The first requirement you should have for a
partner is that *he is available*.** For those of us who
like to pretend we don't know what available means,
here's a definition:

*Available: Free to be in a relationship with you; not
involved with anyone else; not married; not engaged; not
going steady; not sleeping with another person; alone; single; all yours.*

The following are *not* definitions of available:

*With someone, but promises to leave soon
With someone, but he doesn't really love her*

With someone, but they're not having sex anymore
With someone, but says he's just staying for the kids
With someone, but she knows about you and it's all right
With someone, and isn't leaving, but wants you to stick around anyway
Just left someone, but might be going back

In other words, STAY AWAY FROM PEOPLE WHO ARE MARRIED, IN OTHER RELATIONSHIPS, OR TELL YOU THEY AREN'T INTERESTED IN MAKING A COMMITMENT!!!

Until you are emotionally free of the pattern, you might try a Relationship Fast for a while—no dating, no intimate relationships of any kind. This will allow you to become strong in yourself, to spend time healing your old emptiness, and to become clear about the kind of partner you need in your life.

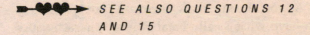 **SEE ALSO QUESTIONS 12 AND 15**

25 *What signs should I look for in the beginning of a relationship to make sure I don't end up with someone who's bad for me?*

I recently ended a really unhealthy relationship that took me years to get out of. I want to start dating again, but I'm so scared that I'll pick another person who will hurt me, and will end up going through the same cycle all over again. How can I tell when I first meet someone if he will be bad for me or not?

━━♥♥➤ I'm so glad you asked! In working with thousands of men and women over the years, I've learned that *so much of the hurt, heartache, and disappointment we experience in love could be avoided if we just paid more attention at the beginning of the relationship.* You need to ask lots of questions, look for the warning signs of potential problems, and stay focused on what you're looking for in a partner and what you are trying to avoid.

As you already know, there are people out there who have what I call "Fatal Flaws," characteristics that can cause severe problems in a relationship. None of us is perfect, and it's obvious that we each have flaws or imperfections that affect our love life. However, some of these characteristics are much more dangerous and destructive than others, and those are the "Fatal Flaws" you need to watch for in a potential partner. Here they are:

1. *Addictions (see Question 23)*

As I've already mentioned, relationships with people who have an addiction (drugs, alcohol, pills, gambling, etc.) are guaranteed to hurt you. Look for signs that there may be problems in this area, and don't minimize what you suspect may be an issue in order to have a relationship with this person, no matter how lonely you are.

2. *Anger*

Living with an angry person is like living with a time bomb: you never know when it's going to go off. Anger is a terrorist—it holds the people it comes in contact with hostage. Spotting someone who has potential problems with anger is one of the easier Fatal Flaws to detect. No one turns into a rage-a-holic overnight. You'll see warning signs: he gets angry when little things don't go his way; he has little patience, and becomes easily annoyed; he has extreme mood swings; he is defensive; he raises his voice often. If you spot these signs, get out before you become the object of his pent-up rage.

3. *Victim Consciousness*

It's often difficult to spot a victim because none of us really minds hearing our partner complain to us about his or her past relationships. *But if your partner has a habit of blaming others for his circumstances and not taking responsibility for his part in problems, watch out: you will be the next person whose fault everything is.* Victims see life as an adversarial situation—"it's the world against me." They ask "Why is this happening to ME?" instead of "Why is this happening and how can I change it?" If you find yourself feeling sorry for a potential mate and getting sucked into his complaints about his life, relationships, health, etc., it's time to leave.

4. *Control Freak*

   A control freak is the opposite of a victim—someone who must make all decisions himself, avoids asking for help, and needs to be in control of his life, and eventually, yours. Don't mistake this Fatal Flaw for the qualities of self-esteem and confidence. Ask yourself if your potential mate's tendency to "take charge" of everything, which may make you temporarily feel taken care of, is really how you want to live. Control freaks will try to talk you out of leaving them, so don't do too much explaining!

5. *Sexual Dysfunction*

   Sexual dysfunction doesn't mean problems only with sexual performance, such as impotence, or inability to have an orgasm. It can also mean sexual obsession, or lack of sexual integrity. This Fatal Flaw is much more difficult to spot at first since (hopefully) you're not having sex on the first few dates, but it can be deadly once you encounter it. You're going to need to have some frank discussion in order to discover whether or not your partner is addicted to fantasy; pornography; compulsive sexual behaviors; throws his sexual energy all over the place; has an aversion to sex due to molestation, rape, or childhood abuse. I know this sounds uncomfortable, but believe me, it's better than finding out about this Fatal Flaw in the middle of a relationship. Some sexual problems aren't necessarily fatal, but they will be if your partner won't deal with them.

6. Your Partner Hasn't Grown Up

Watch out for the charming, childlike person who makes you feel you want to take care of him or her—they may not have grown up enough to have a healthy relationship. Look for signs of financial irresponsibility, someone who is unmotivated, undependable, and avoids taking life seriously. Unless you want to feel like a parent, find someone else.

7. Your Partner Is Emotionally Unavailable

I could write an entire book on this Fatal Flaw. All you need to know is: STAY AWAY FROM PARTNERS WHO ARE EMOTION-ALLY SHUT DOWN! There are so many people in the world eager to love. Why choose someone who has a hard time opening up and spend your time trying to pry open that person's heart? Some people just aren't ready to have a relationship because they are too emotionally blocked. They will have a difficult time talking about or showing emotions, and will resist opening up and trusting. *Find out through frank conversation how comfortable your potential mate is with loving, observe his behavior, and as the relationship progresses, make sure he's capable of giving you what you want before you decide to commit.*

8. Your Partner Hasn't Recovered from Past Relationship(s)

We all carry emotional baggage from our past relationships into each new one. But sometimes that baggage can be so overwhelming that it's fatal to your love affair. *Watch out for someone who still carries tremendous anger and resentment toward his previous mate, someone who feels guilty and responsible for his previous mate, or someone who is still traumatized from being hurt or abused in his past relationships.* It may be this person hasn't healed enough to be ready to love again. Rescuers beware! You will find these kinds of mates very attractive.

9. *Emotional Damage from Childhood*

All of us have some emotional issues originating in our childhood. But some people have emotional damage that is so severe they will have a difficult time having a healthy relationship. This is especially the case when a potential mate isn't aware of the emotional damage and isn't working on himself to repair it. If you meet someone with one of the following issues, that doesn't necessarily mean it will be a Fatal Flaw. It does mean you should be cautious, talk openly about your concerns, and assess how well your partner is dealing with the past or present problems. Here are some of the more dramatic childhood issues that may be warning signs, and should be dealt with:

- Sexual abuse and sexual trauma
- Physical or verbal abuse
- Parental abandonment: divorce, death, adoption, suicide, emotional distance
- Eating disorders
- Parental addiction to alcohol, drugs, etc.
- Religious fanaticism

26 *Can you ever be 100 percent sure that someone you're with is the right one for you? What
qualities should you look for in a partner?*

━━♥♥━► I don't know about 100 percent—nothing in life is certain, because everything is constantly
changing. However, I do believe strongly that if you
learn as much as you can about love, intimacy, and
compatibility, you can be very sure that you have
chosen the right partner. And here's a very important
lesson about compatibility, one that has changed my
life: *The key to choosing the right partner is to look for a
person with good character, not simply a good personality.*

Most of us become initially attracted to a mate
because of something about his or her personality, or
as your question mentioned, "qualities"—his ability
to make you laugh; her softness; his interest in cy-
cling, etc. While these traits might be enjoyable, they
aren't what's going to determine whether or not this
relationship truly makes you happy. For that, you
have to look for character. **Character determines
how a person will treat himself, you, and, one day,
your children. It is the foundation of any healthy
partnership.** If you think of a relationship as a cake,
personality is like the icing, but character is the substance.

It's not enough to ask yourself the question: *Does
my partner love me?* You need to ask a much more important question: *How capable is my partner of loving,
period?* I've found there are six areas you can look at

in a potential partner that define his or her character, and that will help you answer this question and determine how ready this person is to be in a committed relationship.

1. Commitment to Personal Growth

I've listed this characteristic first because I feel it is one of the most important traits to seek in a partner. If you find someone who is committed to their personal growth, you will have already avoided many of the problems couples face: one person wants to work on the relationship and the other doesn't; one partner tries to talk about the issues and the other refuses; one person sees areas that need improvement and the other is in denial.

Commitment to growth means:

- *Your partner is committed to learning everything he can about how to be a better person and a better spouse.*
- *He is willing to receive help and guidance in the form of books, tapes, lectures, seminars, and counseling if necessary.*
- *He is conscious of his blind spots and childhood programming, and is aware of what emotional baggage he has brought into your relationship.*
- *He has personal goals for his own self-improve-*

ment and you can see specific, positive changes in him over time.

2. Emotional Openness

An intimate relationship is not based on sharing a home, a bed, or bathroom. It's based on sharing feelings. That's why the second quality you should look for in a partner is emotional openness. This means your mate:

a. Has feelings

b. Knows *what* he is feeling

c. Chooses to *share* those feelings with you

d. Knows *how* to express those feelings to you

I can't tell you how many excuses I've heard from men and women in unhappy relationships about why their partner cannot express feelings: *IF YOUR PARTNER CANNOT IDENTIFY AND SHARE HIS FEELINGS WITH YOU, HE IS NOT READY TO BE IN AN INTIMATE RELATIONSHIP.*

3. Integrity

Honesty, integrity, and trustworthiness are essential ingredients for a healthy relationship. Knowing that you can count on your partner to be truthful with you at all times will give you a tremendous sense of security. Finding a partner who has integrity means seeking:

- *Someone who is honest with himself.* There are many people who don't lie to you, but lie to themselves. Honesty begins at home, so to speak. *That means you should avoid mates who are masters of self-deception.*

- *Someone who is honest with others.* Does your partner lie to his clients or associates, all in the name of "business"? Does your girlfriend hide the truth about her life from her family? Does your mate often justify doing things at work you feel lack integrity? *If you doubt your partner's integrity, you will lose respect for him,* and it will be difficult for you to trust his behavior toward you.

- *Someone who is honest with you.* That means he will not hide parts of his life or personality from you; he won't tell you only what you want to hear in order to protect himself; he will share the truth with you without your having to trick him into admitting it, or pry it out of him.

- *Someone who doesn't play games.* Games belong on the playground, not in relationships.

4. **Maturity and Responsibility**

Here are some signs that your partner is mature enough to have a relationship:

- *He (or she) can take care of himself.* If your
partner has grown up sufficiently, he'll be
able to earn enough money to support
himself; know how to keep his living space
relatively clean; know how to feed himself.
- *He is responsible. Responsibility means doing
what you say you are going to do.* It means remembering to pay the bills, keeping your
promises, showing up on time, and not letting people down. It isn't a concept—it's
an action.
- *He is respectful.*

5. **High Self-Esteem**

You've probably heard it said before, but
it is true: *YOUR PARTNER CAN ONLY LOVE
YOU AS MUCH AS HE LOVES HIMSELF.*
One of the biggest mistakes we make in
choosing partners is focusing on how much
our mate loves us and how he treats us, and
not how he treats himself. The healthier
your partner's sense of self-esteem, the
stronger your relationship will be. That's
why it's important to look for these signs of
self-esteem:

- *Your partner takes pride in himself.*
      If your mate walks around apologiz-
ing for his life, and seems embarrassed by

who he is, or is constantly putting himself down, then he has no pride in himself. You need a partner who has some extent of satisfaction with who he is now and who he is becoming.

- *Your partner doesn't abuse himself, but takes good care of himself.*

You can tell how someone feels about himself by observing how he treats himself: the food he eats, the environment he lives in, the way he takes care of his body, his car, his possessions. All of these are reflections of self-esteem. Someone who mistreats himself and doesn't mind it won't mind mistreating you either.

- *He doesn't allow others to abuse him.*

Victims are poor choices for partners, even though loving them might make you feel very needed. All the terrible things they complain that others have done to them are merely reflections of their own low self-esteem.

- *He expresses his self-confidence by taking action in his life.*

True self-esteem manifests itself in action. Look for partners who do something about their goals instead of just talking about them.

6. Positive Attitude Toward Life

There is an old saying that goes: *"There are two kinds of people in the world—positive people and negative people."* If you had to spend the rest of your life with one of these kinds, which would you choose? Negative people always focus on problems, find something to complain about, allow worry to rule them, and are cynical. Someone with a positive attitude turns obstacles into opportunities, believes that things can always get better, and focuses on finding solutions.

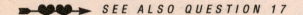 *SEE ALSO QUESTION 17*

Commitment

I am so frustrated that I don't know what to do. I've been living with my partner for seven years, and he still claims he isn't ready to get married to me. I know he loves me, but when I confront him about our future, he tells me he's not ready and needs more time. How long should I be expected to wait for him to make up his mind? I'm thirty-seven years old, and not getting any younger!!

►♥♥► I understand your frustration. You are at that point in a long-term relationship where you and your partner either need to deepen your commitment to one another, or go your separate ways. *A relationship needs to grow in order to last, and commitment gives a relationship purpose and direction and creates a level of safety that, ultimately, brings both partners true emotional freedom.* You know that, and I know that. So what's going on with your boyfriend?

Rather than blaming your mate for "stalling," let's try to understand where he is coming from. Your boyfriend is telling the truth when he says he's not ready to make a commitment. The question you need to ask yourself and him is *"Why aren't you ready?"* **If he doesn't know *the reasons* he's resisting becoming more involved, he can't do anything to improve or heal the situation.** His saying "I don't know what it is" or "I'm working on it" shouldn't be acceptable answers for either of you.

See, for some people "I'm working on it" means "I'll tell you I'm working on it to get you off my back and buy some time because I have no clue what I'm feeling." For others it might mean he is seriously examining his emotional programming in order to understand his fear of commitment. **You need to ask your partner what he means by "I'm working on it."** Ask him *HOW* he is working on it . . . Is he going to therapy, reading books, attending a men's group, talking to other married men? *WHAT SPECIFIC CONCRETE ACTION IS HE TAKING TO WORK ON IT?* What is his goal regarding a time by which he'd like to be clear? A few months? Another year? What is acceptable to you?

There's nothing wrong with a person confronting his fears of intimacy. In fact, it's healthier and more honest than someone who blindly throws himself into a relationship, and then later puts up the emotional walls. I actually feel that a man who says "I'm not ready" might be behaving with incredible honor and respect for you—he doesn't want to propose until he feels right in every part of his being. The problem develops when he's not sure how to get more clear. Maybe he's waiting to wake up one day and find that all his fear has disappeared, but it doesn't usually happen that way. *Fears of commitment come from somewhere, and unless they are examined directly, they may linger forever. They usually involve fear of choosing the wrong partner, fear of turning out like our parents, fear of being hurt, and fear of the unknown.* All of these fears can be resolved by doing some emotional work.

Here's a possibility you need to consider: Sometimes men are afraid to bring up their fears of commitment because the woman in their life seems so *sure,* and he doesn't want to hurt her feelings. It might help to share your own fears about getting married with your boyfriend, so he knows he isn't alone. Perhaps he's been afraid to hurt your feelings by voicing fears like "What if we lose our attraction to one another?" However, if you share your own concern about that issue, and let him know, for example, that you hope to work together with him to make sure to always keep the passion alive, he may find his fear rapidly dissolving.

The following is a powerful exercise I've given to many individuals who have commitment fears. You can suggest that your boyfriend try this—it might help him get in touch with his own feelings about marriage. The exercise has two parts, both fill-in-the-blank. The person taking it should repeat the exercise at least ten times. He can do this out loud with you, or privately with paper and pen:

1. I'll be ready to get married when _____.

Example:
- I own my own home
- I have $50,000 in the bank

- I'm thirty years old
- I never feel turned off by my partner
- I see an example of a happy marriage

2. I'm afraid if we got married_____.

Example:
- You'd leave me like my mother left my father
- I'd feel trapped forever
- I'd never have fun anymore
- I would lose my freedom to have time by my-self
- We'd end up miserable like my parents

Sometimes this exercise reveals issues a person didn't realize were contributing to his fear of marriage. Identifying the fears is always the first step toward healing them. Share my advice with your boyfriend. Hopefully he will feel understood and be willing to work through his fear with you, so you can both go forward to experiencing more love in your lives.

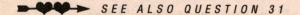 *SEE ALSO QUESTION 31*

28
How soon in a relationship should you expect a commitment from your partner?

My boyfriend and I have been going together for fourteen months. We're both in our early twenties. I feel like I am ready for more of a commitment, but every time I bring it up, he changes the subject or tells me I'm pressuring him. Is this a sign that he's not the one for me? Should I give him an ultimatum to propose or threaten to leave?

━━━━━━━━━━━━━━━━━━━━━━━━━━━━━━━━━━━━━

➧❤❤❤➧ **NO, NO, NO!** *Do not give him an ultimatum. Do not threaten to leave.* Your boyfriend's refusal to propose isn't a sign that he isn't the right one for you—it's a sign that he is thinking more clearly than you are! You've only known each other for a little more than a year. According to my experience, you are just beginning to get into some of the more serious issues that exist in your relationship. Most of the deeper emotional patterns we have don't even begin to surface until about nine months to a year into a relationship. And this is complicated by the fact that you are both still in your early twenties. Trust me—you are going to go through tremendous personal changes in the next five years. If you and he can go through all of this together, and come out stronger and more in love, then you'll know you can create a marriage with a strong foundation. For these reasons, I believe it is way too soon for you to be thinking about marriage.

I'll bet anything your boyfriend is totally conflicted right now. He loves you, probably hopes to spend his life with you, and wants to make you happy, but he intuitively knows that he's not ready to propose. He may not feel confident that he is ready to financially contribute enough to take care of you and a family in the way he would like. He may feel uncertain about his career and need to focus on developing that area of his life before he settles down. On top of that, he's probably scared to death that you will leave him if he doesn't propose. Can you understand what he must be going through?

Now, about that ultimatum you were thinking of giving him. I don't know about you, but I wouldn't feel too thrilled accepting an engagement ring from a man whom I just pressured to propose to me. What's the point? *Forcing him to buy you a ring is manipulative and childish.* You should be more concerned with understanding his feelings, discussing his concerns, and working together to build a stronger, more intimate relationship. Ask him what he thinks of all I've said. Hopefully, he'll look at you with relief and say, "Yes, that's exactly what I've been feeling." Then, you can go forward as a couple committed to love, to truth, and to preparing yourselves for a beautiful life together.

29 Should you stay with someone who isn't over his ex-partner?

My boyfriend is driving me crazy! We've been going out for five months, but he still isn't over his ex-girlfriend. I know they talk on the phone a lot, and last week he took her out for her birthday "just as a friend" because, in his words, "I didn't want her to spend the day alone—she's feeling really vulnerable." When I confront him on this, he accuses me of being possessive and insensitive. Should I just ignore this and hope it goes away?

➤❤❤❤➤ Do you really think if you ignore this problem, it's going to go away? It won't, and you know it. You are in a relationship with someone who is still emotionally attached to his former lover. This is one of the major Fatal Flaws I warn people to look out for when choosing a new mate. (See Question 25.) It's obvious that your boyfriend hasn't let go of his past relationship. *He has all of the classic signs: staying in touch because he is "worried about her"; not setting up proper boundaries with her regarding his new relationship with you; making his concern for her feelings more important than his concern for yours.*

You're in what's called a "triangle" relationship, because there are actually three people involved together. Even when he isn't talking with her, you can feel her presence, can't you? His feelings for her are undoubtedly preventing him from totally surrendering to his relationship with you. It may not be that he actually wants to go back to her—he just might be a rescuer who is having a difficult time letting go of someone without feeling tremendously guilty. Maybe his dad left his mom, and therefore, he has an awful time leaving anyone or anything without feeling like the "bad guy."

Sure, your boyfriend is defensive about his behavior when you confront him, because he doesn't want to confront it himself. *Don't wait for him to wake up and get it. Get out . . . at least for a while.* Let him know that you have come to the conclusion that he hasn't fully detached emotionally from his former girlfriend, and, therefore, isn't ready to be in a committed relationship with anyone else. Tell him how much you care about him, but that you also care about yourself too much to be involved with him right now. Encourage him to take time to decide if he wants to go back with her or not, and invite him to contact you if he is truly ready to love you. Who knows? Your frank discussion may cause him to take a good look at the situation, and he might make a big breakthrough and call you in a few days ready to go forward 100 percent. Or you may never hear from him again. Whatever happens, you will have honored your own needs and feelings, and will win in the end.

➤❤❤➤ *SEE ALSO QUESTIONS 83 AND 96*

Is it right to stay with someone even when you know inside she's not the right one for you?

I'm in a terrible situation. I've been living with a wonderful woman for two years, and I know she is madly in love with me and wants to get married, but I don't feel the same way. I love her, and we have a great time together, but I've always known she's not "the one" I want to spend the rest of my life with. I don't want to hurt her by telling her this, and it seems so foolish to break up when we are doing so well. What's the right thing for me to do?

➤❤❤❤➤ Let me get this straight—you are living with a woman who's crazy about you, but you know she's not enough for you, so you continue to lead her on and give her hope by staying when you secretly long to leave . . . and you call this "doing so well"? Maybe you're doing well, but she's doing terribly, or at least she would be if she knew that the man she adores doesn't feel the same way about her. *I know you claim you don't want to hurt her, but the truth is that every minute you steal from her life is hurting her; every moment when she lies next to you, believing she is safe and secure in your love is hurting her; every time you selfishly decide to stay one more week or year since you're enjoying yourself, knowing that you're staying on false pretenses, you're hurting her.*

This woman wants the same thing most women want: to find a partner she can trust to love, honor, and cherish her, and to live with that person happily and faithfully for the rest of her life. Believe me, your girlfriend never secretly dreamt that, one day, she'd meet a man who would mislead her into believing she'd finally found her soul mate, only to discover after several years that he'd known all along she wasn't "the one," but never got around to telling her. That is every woman's nightmare, not every woman's fantasy.

You say "it seems foolish to break up." Let me ask you: foolish to whom? To you? Why should you give up a comfortable situation before you have to? Is that what you consider foolish? Do you think if your girlfriend knew how you felt, she would agree that it would be "foolish" to end the relationship? I'll bet that she would have other, less polite words to say to you, and that the only time she'd use the word "foolish" would be in describing how she felt living with a man for two years, yet never suspecting that he had no intentions of ever marrying her.

If this answer sounds harsh, it is intended to be. *Would you want someone to do this same thing to you? I think not. So do what is right and honorable. Tell her the truth, now, and leave.* Sorry . . . there's no way to leave and have her not feel angry and betrayed. That's your karma. And don't delude yourself into believing that by staying, you will avoid hurting her. First of all, not hurting her has never been your motivation for being there; fulfilling your own, selfish needs has been your true agenda. And second, know that she will one day tell people that "the nicest thing he ever did for me was to walk out the door." Please, take some time to examine your own heart and soul before you get involved with another woman.

31 How can you tell if someone is really committed to the relationship?

My partner claims he really loves me and wants to be with me, but when it comes to working on "us," he continually disappoints me. Whenever I bring up what I'm unhappy with, or ask him for some things I need from him in order to stay together, he apologizes and promises to change. If I press him further, he gets defensive and says "I'm working on it." The point is, nothing has changed, and I'm afraid it never will, but I know he really does love me, and I don't want to lose him. How can I tell if he is serious about this relationship?

First of all, read the answer to Question 14, because it applies to your situation. This will help you understand how to ask him if he is serious about the relationship, and if he wants the same kind of relationship you do. If he insists that he does, and that he truly wants to change, *you need to address two major issues: 1) What commitments you need from him; and 2) HOW he plans to work on himself so that he can fulfill those commitments.*

I have a feeling that, in your case, your mate really means it when he says he wants to be with you and work on things. *The problem may be that he doesn't fully understand WHAT he needs to work on and doesn't have a clue as to HOW to work on these issues.* At the risk of sounding sexist, I must say that I have seen this situation countless times with men whose wives or girlfriends complain of the same frustrations you do. Often, these men are too proud or embarrassed to say to their women *"Look, I know I need to change, but to be honest with you, I have no idea exactly what you want me to change, and even less of an idea of how I would actually make these mysterious changes."* Instead, they say "I'm working on it," or "Stop pressuring me," hoping to buy enough time to figure out what the hell they're supposed to do.

If you're a woman reading this, you're probably thinking, "Come on, Barbara, what's so complicated about wanting your husband to be more intimate, or share more of his feelings? How hard can it be for him to understand these requests?" My answer is: *much harder than you could ever imagine!!* Most women are much more familiar with their inner world of feelings than are most men; we naturally understand what it means to "open up," or "let someone in," or "surrender to the moment." However, to many men, these concepts are strange, and even frightening.

I've discovered that the more verbally clear and specific women are in defining exactly what behaviors they would like their partners to develop, and the more concrete tools they offer their partners to assist them in making those changes, the more willing men are to actually "work on it."

Here is an exercise from my Making Love Work Program that has helped hundreds of thousands of couples learn how to work on improving their relationship. In particular, I've received wonderful feedback from men who shared how this exercise allowed them to truly understand what their wives needed and gave them ideas for how they could specifically fulfill those needs.

On one side of a piece of paper, list all the things you need from your partner, the ways you'd like him to change. Then, in the second column next to each item, write down specifically how he could demonstrate his commitment to fulfilling that need.

EXAMPLE:

What I Need	How You Could Demonstrate It
I need him to be more emotionally open with me about his feelings.	Tell me what's bothering you before I have to ask a bunch of times, even if it's a little thing you think isn't important.
	Tell me you love me sometimes first, before I say it.
	Reach out to take my hand when we are walking somewhere instead of waiting for me to reach out to you first.

You'd be amazed at how powerful this process is. Often the man will respond by saying *"Oh, is that what you mean by being open? I can do that."* And you think to yourself, "What took you so long?" Perhaps he was missing the HOW of "working on it." Naturally, both partners should do the above exercise. Suggest this to your mate. Hopefully, it will provide him with the tools he was looking for to give you what you wanted and, as an added bonus, to even express some of his own needs. Once this works, you'll find your partner is much less defensive about the idea of changing, and you can go on to exploring other methods of transformation together—tapes, seminars, counseling, etc.

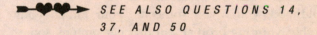 *SEE ALSO QUESTIONS 14, 37, AND 50*

I keep going through the same frustrating cycle in my relationships. When I first meet someone I'm attracted to, I really want to get close, and I appear very loving and open to my partner. But the more the other person wants some kind of commitment, the more I pull away, until one day, I leave. My last lover accused me of being a "commitment phobic." How can I tell if I'm just going through a normal selection process, or if I have a serious problem?

➤❤❤➤ Sounds suspicious to me!! If this has happened over and over again, you almost certainly do have "commitment phobia." **That would make you what I call a "Commitment Rebel."** If in your childhood, you loved someone, your father, your mother, your big brother, but that person took something from you—your power, your self-esteem, your innocence, your voice, you may unconsciously have thought of that person as "the enemy," even though you loved them. *So when you grow up and you meet a partner and you love that person, automatically in your mind, you think "people I love are the enemy. They want something from me. I have to hold my ground,"* and you will have a hard time committing to that person. This resistance to commitment might express itself in major ways, such as actually refusing to commit to marriage, or it might express itself in small ways, such as refusing to commit to going to counseling, or not taking out the garbage when you said you would.

Commitment Rebels are motivated by a need to be in control, and a fear of losing control. Committing to someone will feel like you're giving something up, as if they won and you lost. That's because in some earlier relationship, it did feel like you lost something by loving that person who hurt you.

Here are some characteristics of Commitment Rebels. If you're one, you will recognize these. (If you're in love with one, you'll race into the other room to show your partner what I wrote!)

1. *Commitment Rebels don't like being told what to do.*
   They can become easily defensive and argumentative.

2. *Commitment Rebels are often irresponsible with time and money.*
   They may be late a lot, not pay bills on time.

3. *Commitment Rebels don't like making plans.*
   They resist committing to the future or pinning themselves down.

4. *Commitment Rebels don't like talking about or showing feelings.*

It feels like too much of a commitment, and gives the other person too much power.

5. *Commitment Rebels are often procrastinators.*
They don't like committing to doing anything in particular.

6. *Commitment Rebels can be unmotivated with no strong direction in life.*
They are afraid to commit even to their dreams.

Naturally, a Commitment Rebel will panic the moment his partner starts using the "C" word, as you have in all of your relationships. So what's the solution? First, I suggest you go on a Relationship Fast. That doesn't mean having lots of fast relationships, but the opposite: no dating or intimate involvement with *anyone* for a while. Pull all your energies back on yourself so you can break this pattern. Next, do some serious work on healing your emotional programming. (See Questions 12 and 15.) *Within every Commitment Rebel is a hurt and angry little child who felt very controlled when he was small. You need to help that child take his power back from whomever you feel took it from him.* You can do this with a really good and qualified therapist, a program like Making Love Work, or in whatever manner you choose. Once you finish that unfinished emotional business from your childhood, you will be free for the first time in your life to love as deeply as you want to love.

➤➤❤❤❤➤   *SEE ALSO QUESTIONS 12 AND 15*

33

Is there such a thing as falling in love too quickly? What does it mean if a person experiences this often?

I'm madly in love with my boyfriend, and we're talking about getting married. My friends think I'm crazy, since we've only known each other for about six weeks, but our relationship is perfect! The only thing that makes me a little nervous is that in the past, I have been engaged or lived with two other men, both within the first three months of meeting them. Am I falling in love too fast? How do I slow down?

➤♥♥♥➤ You are a bona fide *"Love-at-first-sight junkie"*!! You are addicted to falling in love, and the instant high it gives you, especially in the beginning of the relationship. Love-at-first-sight junkies are in love with love, and it doesn't usually take much for you to feel it. Once you get hooked on a new partner, your mental faculties seem to all but disappear, and you say things like "our relationship is perfect" when the truth is, you hardly know the person. And that's the point. You don't really *want* to know him, because if you did, you'd have to take him off of his pedestal and see him as a flawed human being, and that would ruin your fantasy.

I wouldn't even call what you're doing "falling in love." It may be more like "falling in lust," or an infatuation with who you think the other person is. *You are so commitment hungry that you are looking for a commitment rather than looking for a good relationship.* True, some people do know the moment they meet their partner that it is right, but in your case, you've made a profession of instant love affairs, so I am pretty sure this isn't the real thing. And the problem is that once the relationship does become more real, and you are forced to deal with all of the challenges every couple faces, you become disenchanted, feel like you've "fallen out of love," and break it off, right?

There are two issues you need to deal with. First, why you keep doing this, and second, what to do about your present situation. Let's talk about the why. Love-at-first-sight junkies are usually people with very wounded hearts. I know—I used to be one. *When you were small, you probably did not have the loving family you wanted, and in some way felt rejected, abandoned, or not good enough. You grow up with this huge, unfulfilled desire to belong, to have someone, anyone, there for you, to fill the emptiness you've carried inside you for as long as you can remember.* And it doesn't take much to fill this order. A person comes along, usually someone who is also desperate to feel wanted, and you latch onto each other like two drowning sailors who just discovered a plank of wood floating in the ocean.

If you ever want to have a truly healthy and lasting relationship, and I know you do, you are going to have to face the demon you've run from your whole life: your pain. You're in need of intense emotional healing work (see Questions 12 and 15). Stop hiding behind your infatuations, and find the courage to look within. There you will find the answers to all your questions and, ultimately, the love you've been seeking.

Now, about your boyfriend. You don't necessarily have to break up with him. Hopefully, you can both do this emotional work together, and actually begin to create a real relationship. **But whatever you do, do not live together and do not get married.** Don't even talk about it. Slow down. Date each other, and get to know yourself, as well as the other person. Day by day, week by week, your relationship will grow, slowly, like a tree sprouting from a seed, planting its roots firmly in the soil.

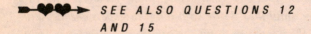 *SEE ALSO QUESTIONS 12 AND 15*

34 Should you wait until you are 100 percent sure that someone is right for you before you make a lifelong commitment?

My partner and I have been together for four years, and are talking about getting married. We have a very loving relationship, and are best friends, but we both want to be really sure before we get engaged. The problem is that there are moments when she does something that annoys me, and I wonder whether I'm making a mistake, and she admits she has occasional doubts too. Her parents were divorced, and mine had a loveless marriage, so we really want to be careful. Should we wait until we are 100 percent sure all the time before we make a commitment?

➡️💕💕➡️ If you were sure 100 percent of the time that your relationship was perfect, with no moments when you became annoyed or upset, I would dub both you and your partner saints!! It is natural to have doubts, especially when both of your parents had dysfunctional relationships, and when we live in a society with such a high divorce rate. And as any happily married couple can tell you, even after you commit totally, there will be moments when you are so upset with your partner that you think to yourself, "I knew it—I made a mistake." Fortunately, those moments pass and are replaced with the love and friendship that is the foundation of the relationship.

My point is this: I don't believe that in our uncertain world, we are ever 100 percent certain 100 percent of the time about anything. None of us knows what the future holds, and if we think seriously about this, it may be difficult to make a commitment to marriage, if we believe that means we are promising someone how we will feel at a future date. "What if in twenty years, my husband and I have grown apart because he stops loving me?" you think to yourself. "How can I be sure that won't happen?" The answer is that you can't—you can both only do the best you can to make sure your relationship stays healthy and passionate every day.

I hear your concern about making a mistake, and wanting some kind of ultimate reassurance that you are indeed doing the right thing. It's as if you would like God to come down and say, **"Hi there. Listen, I know you've been wondering whether you should marry your boyfriend or not. Let me reassure you that he is indeed the one I had in mind for you, so trust me, you're not making a mistake. Feel better now? Good. Gotta run. Lots to do in heaven. Bye-bye."** Whew! Now that God told you you're making the right choice, you can relax.

Unfortunately, we don't get that kind of supreme reassurance about our love choices. Read Questions 10, 17, and 26 for more clarity about compatibility, talk about every issue you need to discuss, and if you feel confident that you are right for one another, don't allow those tiny doubts that pop up once in a while to keep you from taking a leap into your future together. *(Obviously, more than a little doubt may be a warning sign from your heart that you are not making the right choice, as we've discussed earlier.)* And guess what? There will be a surprise waiting for you when you do make that commitment to spend your lives together—just the act of committing alone will have magically erased all kinds of small concerns you had, and you'll find yourselves more in love than ever!

◆❤❤➤ *SEE ALSO QUESTIONS 10, 17, 25, AND 26*

My girlfriend and I have been dating for a few years and are starting to talk seriously about our future. She wants to get married right away, but I still have some doubts and fears about the relationship. I've suggested living together as a next step, but she's afraid it will somehow ruin things between us. What's your opinion of a couple living together before marriage?

►●●● ► In the past few decades, millions of couples of all ages have chosen to live together, either as a prelude to marriage, or in place of marriage. *(NOTE: If you have strong judgments about living together due to your religious or moral beliefs, please understand that I'm looking at this issue purely from a psychological point of view, and skip this question if you wish.)* I feel it's important to understand both the positive and negative consequences of living with someone you love.

THE CASE FOR LIVING TOGETHER:

There is a part of me that feels, after having seen so many dysfunctional and incompatible relationships over the years, all couples should live together before deciding to get married. I wonder how many unhealthy relationships would have ended if the two partners had tried being together twenty-four hours a day, and thus had come face to face with the issues they were avoiding by seeing each other only on weekends or a few nights a week.

Here are some of the benefits of living together:

1. **You discover sides of your partner's personality you cannot know about unless you live together**. There is no way you can get to know a person whom you see intermittently as well as if you lived together. It's a lot easier for someone to be on his best behavior for three hours during a date than it is for him to maintain that behavior day after day when you live under the same roof. When you live with someone, you uncover habits, attitudes, and behaviors you never see otherwise. You see him in his natural habitat, his home, and thus become exposed to sides of his personality he may be hiding from you when he is outside in the world. You see him when he is tired, when he is sick, when he is angry, when he is frustrated, and when he is grumpy. **You get exposure to the full range of his or her emotional reactions.**

   I've heard so many nightmare stories about people marrying and moving in together, only to discover things about each other that are unacceptable. Marriage is tough enough without any unpleasant surprises.

2. **You discover more about whether or not your lifestyles are truly compatible.** Some men make great lovers in a romantic affair, but lousy husbands. Some women are fantastic part-time companions, but terrible full-time wives. *You may enjoy loving someone, but hate living with him.* The qualities that encourage you to fall in love with someone and have a great time seeing him may not be enough to create day-to-day harmony once you move in together. You may find out your partner's lifestyle doesn't fit with yours, something you'd never know about unless you shared the same living space over a long period of time.

3. **You discover how capable your partner is of true partnership.** Living together requires a sharing of power and control; it demands compromise and flexibility from both partners since you are merging the habits and desires of two unique individuals. You may not find out how willing or capable your mate is of true partnership until you commit to living together. *Only when you have to make decisions together about finances, food, household responsibilities, acquisitions, etc. do you truly discover what kind of team player your partner is.*

THE CASE AGAINST LIVING TOGETHER:

1. **You can destroy the relationship by expecting too much from it when it's still developing.** Although I personally feel living together with a mate can be a valuable experience at a certain stage of the relationship, I also feel that *living together prematurely is a big mistake.* I've counseled too many couples who moved in together for the wrong reasons:

   - To save money
   - Because one had a nicer place
   - So they could spend more time together
   - Because one partner was afraid of losing the other

   Living together before your relationship has reached a significant level of commitment, maturity, and emotional stability can actually speed up the disintegration of the relationship. If your relationship isn't ready to handle the pressures of living together, it might fall apart under the strain that living together prematurely brings.

2. **You can become emotionally lazy.** If moving in with someone feels like a goal to you, and

you live together before you're ready, you risk becoming emotionally lazy in the relationship. You may avoid conflict in order to keep the peace, especially if you haven't learned to work through conflict together. You may give your partner less attention and appreciation since he or she is there all the time, or neglect the relationship in other ways.

3. **You can avoid furthering your commitment to one another.** You may have heard the saying *"Why buy the cow when you can get the milk for free?"* I think it was used by many of our mothers in their attempt to convince us that boys wouldn't marry us if we had sex with them, since they were already getting what they wanted. I've heard this same argument about living together—**that if a man is living with you and enjoying the benefits of domestic life, he has no reason to ask you to marry him.** I have to agree that in some cases, not all, this may be true, especially if you haven't known one another for a good length of time. *Some commitment phobic men (or women) might hide behind living together in order to still experience the intimacy they crave, but also to avoid making the final commitment of marriage.*

I don't believe the solution is to refuse to move in with someone unless you are engaged or married, unless that feels right to you. *If you are considering living with someone, but want the formal structure of marriage somewhere down the road, you need to discuss all of this before you actually move in together in order to avoid any misunderstandings. You may want to come up with a time projection, nine months or a year, for instance, at which point you will reevaluate your relationship and decide whether or not you feel ready to marry.*

Communication
and
Conflict

36 *How can I get my partner to express his feelings to me?*

I know my husband loves me, but he never expresses it verbally. He comes from a family that isn't very communicative, and claims "words don't mean much to him." How can I get him to express his feelings to me? I'm starving for some attention.

━━◆◆◆━━ You're what I call "word-hungry," starving to hear verbal expressions of your husband's love that will fill up your heart. Like all of us, your husband formed his love habits at an early age, and obviously didn't experience being loved with *words, nor see examples of his parents using words to express feelings. Remember—he's not withholding verbal affection on purpose; he simply doesn't understand why it is so important to you, or how to fulfill your needs. So let's* talk about how you can explain this to him so he gets it!!

One of the best ways to create intimate connections between you and your beloved is with **words**. *Words are* bridges *that allow you to travel from your private world into your partner's.* They link your silences together, so you can know the person you love from the inside out, and he can know you. They give your mind evidence to trust what your heart already knows. Deep inside, you *feel* he loves you but when you hear him say those words, the experience becomes that much more real.

Some people argue that words, by definition, cannot possibly contain the fullness of emotion, and therefore limit your experience of intimacy. "Talking about it trivializes the love," they insist. I strongly disagree—**without words to make the feelings tangible and transferable, the feelings will not be as real to you or to your partner.** Words stir up the love energy between you. They are like the wind, making waves upon the ocean of feeling you share. The water is always there in the sea, but it is the wind that moves it, teasing it from stillness until it rises into sparkling swells. Your feelings are always there in your heart, but it is the words that give them movement from silence into expression.

Many lovers are stingy with their words. They hoard them as if there are a limited number of "*I love you's*," "*I need you's*," and "*You make me so happy's*" available, and they don't want to use them up. So they conserve the amount of verbal love they share, saving it for special occasions such as birthdays or anniversaries, and leave their partner feeling hungry for words the majority of the time. Whenever I've confronted verbally stingy men in my life, they always responded with this defensive reasoning for why they weren't loving me more with words:

"*If I say it all the time, it won't mean anything anymore . . .*" This thinking is as absurd as believing that if you wear a beautiful dress often, it won't be as beautiful as if you only wear it once in a while, or that if you kiss your little girl or boy good night *every night* and tell them you love them, it won't mean as much as if you only do it once every four months!

The result of this kind of emotional stinginess will be that the mate who isn't hearing love words feels controlled and resentful, and that's what you're feeling now. Your partner has been putting you on a "verbal love diet" without realizing it. You need more words of love from your husband—**they will feed your heart and nourish your spirit.**

Translating feelings into words isn't always easy. Some of us, like your husband, aren't very familiar with the language of love, because no one ever used it with us. *"I don't like talking about feelings—that's just the way I am,"* we claim. Some of us feel uncomfortable using words, either because we fear we aren't very good with them, or because expressing our emotions in words leaves us feeling vulnerable and unprotected. *"I'm not sure what to say. I just can't describe it,"* or *"I don't want to talk about it,"* we protest. **But I believe that our fear or lack of ability is no excuse for not learning how to use words to be a better lover.**

Share my thoughts with your husband. (And for all you other women out there, place this book open to this page in front of your lover when needed!) **Perhaps when he understands that you're not asking him to put feelings into words to get him to do things "your way," but want to appreciate his love**

for you even more than you already do, he'll be
willing to try using more words. And don't forget to
remind him that women get turned on in our heads
first, and that, for most of us, loving words are a
powerful aphrodisiac!!

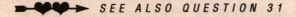   SEE ALSO QUESTION 31

37 What do you do with a husband who refuses to discuss problems or work on the relationship?

Trying to get through to my husband is like banging my head against a steel wall. He refuses to discuss our problems, tells me they are my issues, and says if I want to read books or go to therapy, I should go ahead, but to leave him out of it. This has been going on for years. Our marriage is in major trouble, but he doesn't want to see it, and I feel like saving it is up to me. Is this something that I can do alone? Is there something that I can do to wake him up?

➡️💕💕💕➡️ This is one of the saddest questions I have heard over and over again throughout my career. A husband or wife approaches me tearfully and shares a story like yours of a marriage that is in severe trouble, and a partner who absolutely refuses to discuss any problems. You may not like my answer, but here goes: *You are not presently in a marriage.* What do I mean by that? I mean that marriage is not a living arrangement, or how many years you have been together, or a piece of paper that says you are husband and wife. Marriage is ultimately the commitment to loving your partner and doing everything you can to make the relationship work.

Since your husband refuses to face or discuss your problems, and will not agree to any outside help in solving your conflicts, he has broken his commitment to your relationship as much as if he had an affair. He may be scared; he may have had an abusive childhood; he may have a wonderful, loving heart somewhere inside of him. The fact remains that, unless he is willing to be an *active participant* in your partnership, there is no partnership. *And you can't make a marriage work alone.* (See Questions 3, 12, 14, and 31.)

I believe there are five commitments every marriage needs to survive and grow. These are commitments both partners should make:

1. *I am committed to learning everything I can about being a better person and a better mate, and I will do whatever it takes to make the relationship work.*

2. *I am committed to being emotionally open to and with my partner by sharing my feelings.*

3. *I am committed to being emotionally generous with my partner, not emotionally stingy, and will express my love and affection.*

4. *I am committed to being honest with my partner and myself.*

5. *I am committed to learning how to love my partner as much as he or she truly deserves to be loved.*

Frankly, I don't know how any relationship can be truly healthy without these commitments. Take Commitment #1, for instance, the one you and your husband are struggling with right now. If a partner isn't committed to doing whatever it takes to make the relationship work, what's the point of being in a relationship at all? Being committed to merely living in the same house with you and calling you a wife does not qualify as being a good husband. A good husband, or wife, fights for the marriage, and will try everything, until it's obvious that nothing is going to work.

Apparently, you've tried to get through to your husband countless times. Try once more, and use this analogy. Ask him to imagine that one of your children, or a beloved pet, had been hit by a car and was lying, bleeding, in the street. Would your husband say "I don't believe in hospitals," and leave your loved one there to die? Would he stubbornly refuse to get help? I don't think so. He'd rush the person he loved to the hospital and beg for all the help he could get. Well, guess what? *Your relationship is lying, bleeding, in the street. If it doesn't get help, it's going to die.* Ask him one more time. If he truly refuses to participate in an effort to save it, if he stubbornly holds his ground, know that it is time for you to leave before you, too, bleed to death emotionally.

➡️💜➡️ SEE ALSO QUESTIONS 3, 12, 14, AND 31

38 *How can I get over my fear of conflict and be more honest with my partner?*

When I was young, there was a lot of yelling and drama in my house, and I vowed I'd never turn out like my parents, especially my mother who was a raging alcoholic with major mood swings. The result is that I am scared to death of conflict, and try to "keep the peace," but I end up holding back a lot of my feelings from my partner. What can I do to overcome my fear of anger?

You're describing one of the deadliest mistakes people make in their relationships: they push down all the "not nice" feelings because they don't want to rock the boat, and by doing so, they end up destroying their emotional connection and killing the passion. I can't tell you how many couples I've worked with who were on the verge of divorce, all because *they had tried so hard to avoid any conflict or confrontation, and thus, never had a chance to resolve any of the issues in their relationship.* The good news is that you're aware of what you're doing and have the chance to make new, healthy decisions about how you handle unpleasant emotions.

I'm going to give you a fairly extensive answer to your question, because this is a serious problem that so many people are challenged by, and it's crucial that you understand what you can to do change your situation.

First, I encourage you to do some serious work

on healing your emotional programming (see Question 12). This is how I see it: Sometime when you were a child, you made some unconscious emotional decisions such as *"If I feel angry, I'll be bad like my mother,"* or *"It's not safe for me to express my feelings."* These decisions are still running your life years later. Consciously, you know you aren't your mother, yet you've made strict rules for yourself to make sure you never behave in a way that remotely resembles her abuse. So when your partner does something that upsets you, and you feel the natural response of irritation or anger, alarm bells go off in your brain that warn "Danger!! Danger!!" and you instinctively suppress those angry feelings before they can surface.

Here's what I'd like you to think about: **The danger you're perceiving does not have its source in present time. It's the danger you felt as a child when your mother became angry, because you weren't sure how she was going to behave.** Whenever you encounter anger, yours, your mate's, or anyone's for that matter, the old unresolved emotions of terror are triggered. It's as if that five-year-old child is in charge of your emotional life. Healing your emotional programming means doing some work where you give that child part of you a chance to find her voice and say all the "not nice" things she didn't feel safe saying when she was little. You, as her adult "parent," need to communicate with that inner child, assuring her that she is safe, that it's okay for her to express herself, and that she has permission to be upset. It will also help if your mate verbally gives you permission to not always be nice, and to express your angry feelings (appropriately, of course).

The second part of the solution has to do with understanding the nature of anger so you won't be so frightened by it. One of the basic concepts I teach is called *The Emotional Map*. The Emotional Map is a simple yet powerful formula to help you understand your own feelings and the feelings of others, and to assist you in moving out of unpleasant emotions, such as anger, hurt, or fear and back to a state of love.

According to the Emotional Map, we are always experiencing our emotions in layers. These six levels of feelings are:

1. *ANGER, Blame, and Resentment*

2. *HURT, Sadness, and Disappointment*

3. *FEAR, Insecurity, and Emotional Wounds*

4. *REGRET, Understanding, and Responsibility*

5. *INTENTION, Solutions, and Wishes*

6. *LOVE, Forgiveness, and Appreciation*

Here is an example of how the Emotional Map works. Let's say my husband does something that makes me really angry. Anger is simply the most obvious emotion I'm feeling. Underneath the anger, I am hurt. When someone hurts us enough, we feel anger as an unconscious means of protecting ourselves. So I'm not just feeling "I'm furious at you for being two hours late," I'm also feeling HURT: "It really hurt me that you were so insensitive to my feelings." Underneath the hurt, I'm feeling something even deeper and more basic—FEAR. This is the level of emotion where all of our old emotional wounds are stored, that place where the frightened child gets triggered. So along with my anger, and hurt, I am also feeling, "I'm afraid you'll always work so hard that we won't have enough time together. And this reminds me of how I felt waiting for my father to come home at night when he wouldn't show up."

Do you follow what's happening so far? Even though I started out feeling really angry, anger was just the tip of the iceberg, so to speak. When I delve deeper into my emotions, the source of much of my anger is a lot of fear, some from the present, and some left over from the past. The fourth level of the map is called REGRET, and understanding. Once I take a look at my fears, my wounds and what's really triggering my reaction, I can begin to see the whole picture and understand more of what is going on. Perhaps I also have regrets about how I lashed out with my anger, or how I didn't say anything, but was cold to my husband that evening. Now I'm moving toward resolving my feelings. And the next level deeper down is INTENTION—what I want to happen, my solutions, my hopes. "I want us to work this out. I'd like you to call next time you are late."

What is the deepest and sixth level of feeling in our Emotional Map? LOVE, of course, and forgiveness. *If I didn't love my husband so much, I wouldn't be mad in the first place.* It's because I love him that I became afraid, then hurt, and eventually, hurt enough to be angry. This is why I say: "*Anger is love turned inside out.*" When you resolve your upset feelings and communicate using the Emotional Map to take you back to love, that is called communicating *The Complete Truth.*

I've taken the time to explain this in hopes that you are beginning to understand three important points:

1) **Angry emotions aren't "bad"—they are a natural result of feeling the love being blocked, and are only dangerous when they are acted out, instead of talked out.**

2) **When you suppress your anger, you end up suppressing all of the emotions underneath it, thus cutting yourself off from the love.**

3) **When you're unable to resolve your angry feelings in a constructive way, those emo-**

tions don't just disappear—you store those feelings inside of you. *"Outrage that isn't expressed becomes In-rage."* Can you imagine how much energy it takes to hold down all that anger? When you're suppressing anger you may find yourself feeling tired, lifeless, hopeless. You're using up your vital energy to keep the anger from showing.

I've given you a lot to think about. Start practicing communicating the complete truth about a small issue, and see how well it works! (For more information on this technique, see *How to Make Love All the Time,* or the Making Love Work Program.)

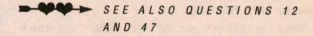 *SEE ALSO QUESTIONS 12 AND 47*

39 How important is it for a couple to be totally honest with one another? Is there such a thing as too much honesty?

▬━♥♥♥━► Whenever I hear this question, I know that the person asking it has something he or she does not want to be honest about with a partner, perhaps something he or she fears will jeopardize the relationship. So I'll cut to the chase. How important is it for a couple to be totally honest in their relationship? *It is crucially important.* (See Question 38.) Each time you withhold a truth from your partner, you have to push those feelings down, and eventually, you end up feeling emotionally numb. "I guess I just fell out of love," you tell yourself, but the truth is, you built a wall between yourself and the love by not communicating the truth.

Now regarding your concern about "too much honesty"—most of the time that phrase refers to the very important feelings you need to share the most with your partner, such as:

> *"I don't like the way you touch me when we make love."*
>
> *"I'm feeling attracted to other people, and I know that means I'm not getting enough of what I need from you."*
>
> *"I hate the way you put me down all the time. It has to stop."*

> *"I resent how much time you give your work, yet
> you never plan time for us."*

Once in a while, I will meet someone who is "too honest." This person uses the pretense of extreme honesty to make people uncomfortable, to control their loved ones, and to cover up their own fears and insecurities. For instance, saying the following would be, in my opinion, too much, or more accurately, unnecessary, honesty:

> *"You know, honey, your hair turned out terribly
> today. You don't look very attractive."*
> *"Jimmy, your sister's school grades are much higher
> than yours. I'm beginning to think you're not
> the smart son I hoped for."*
> *"Marilyn, I'm happy that you finally have a
> boyfriend, but don't you think he's kind of on
> the ugly side?"*

Now, technically, these comments may reflect the truth. But the point is, what is the purpose of expressing these feelings? Is it essential to the health of your relationship with the person? Will communicating about these issues resolve anything? The answer, of course, is "NO." These are examples of hurtful criticism or insensitivity disguised as honesty.

I know how scary it is to be honest with someone you love, especially when you aren't sure how he or she will react. But the alternative is even more frightening—pushing your feelings down, living in denial, and ending up emotionally dead. Find the courage to honor your truth and communicate in a way it can be heard.

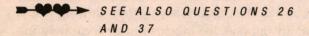 *SEE ALSO QUESTIONS 26 AND 37*

*I have a problem I'm embarrassed to admit to: I have a re-
ally bad temper that is ruining my love life. It doesn't take
much to set me off, and I end up taking my anger out on my
mate, my children, even strangers. What's wrong with me?
How can I learn to control myself?*

➤➤♥♥♥➤ First of all, I'm proud of you for having
the courage to take responsibility for your behavior,
instead of blaming it on everyone else in your life
and insisting that "they make you angry." I wish
more people would admit that they have a problem
with inappropriate anger—the world would be a
much nicer and safer place in which to live! And
you're right, your anger is ruining your life. *A person
who is prone to anger causes his or her friends and family
to live in constant fear, and fear is the enemy of love.*

Let's examine the two questions you asked:
"What's wrong with me?" and "How can I learn to
control myself?" First of all, nothing is "wrong" with
you; something is wrong *inside of you.* **You aren't a
bad person because you are angry. You are probably
angry because, when you were a child, you were
treated like or felt like a bad person.**

Haven't you noticed that often you get upset
over insignificant things; that events that shouldn't
have such a powerful effect on you set you off? That's
because the source of most of your anger is not found

in the present, but in the past. Most rage-a-holics, and that describes you, experienced one or all of the following circumstances while they were growing up:

- *They were physically, verbally, or sexually abused as a child* and stored up the rage inside, letting it out as an adult when they finally feel "safe."
- *They felt unloved or abandoned as a child,* either through divorce, an absent parent, the death of a parent and act out that childhood rage as adults when they meet people who love them (potential "leavers").
- *They felt powerless as a child*—they had alcoholic parents they couldn't save; they watched helplessly as one parent abused the other; they never had permission to express their feelings, and, as adults, they compensate for that powerlessness by controlling others with their anger.

If a child experiences any of the situations I just mentioned, he will naturally feel enormous sadness and grief. If he is unable to feel that grief, or doesn't have permission to express it, or the angry feelings accompanying it, it will surface years later as inappropriate anger and rage. Many adults who appear angry are simply acting out repressed grief from their childhoods.

This brings us to your second question, regarding your desire to "control your anger." Learning to control your anger will not solve your problem. The anger is a symptom, albeit a totally unacceptable symptom, of a rage-a-holic's deep hurt and sadness. **Just treating the anger without understanding the cause will be a very temporary and dangerous solution.**

Sure, you can learn to count to ten, to take time-outs, all useful methods for learning to communicate your feelings appropriately. But I believe you must also work on locating and healing the source of the anger, and give that hurt little child permission to express the emotions he's been holding in all his life. You know my saying: **"If you don't work it out, you'll act it out."**

Even traditional talk or psychotherapy may not be an adequate form of help for someone suffering from chronic anger. Supervised experiential emotional work such as psychodrama, physical forms of release such as hitting punching bags, screaming into pillows and using batakas to strike out, and intensive inner-child work will all be essential ingredients in helping a person transform his anger into grief and, finally, into healing. Once you begin to release the old, pent-up emotions, you will find that "controlling your anger" becomes much easier, since you won't feel the anger as frequently, and therefore won't react from an angry place. Naturally, you can employ other techniques like "time-outs," etc., which a qual-

ified therapist can teach you, while you're in the
process of doing your deeper work. Remember: By
facing and healing your old demons, you're not only
giving your loved ones a wonderful gift, but you're
loving yourself in the most profound way possible.

➤♥♥♥➤ *SEE ALSO QUESTIONS 12*
               AND 38

41 *Why do my wife and I fight all the time? How can we stop?*

It seems like my wife and I fight all the time. It doesn't even matter what the issues are—we're constantly at each other's throats. I know we love each other, and we want to stop, but our truces last for a day at the most, and then we're back to bickering. What's going on?

━━◆◆◆━━ You said the magic phrase: "It doesn't even matter what the issues are," and you're right. This is one of the most important concepts to understand about conflict in relationships. The most common issues couples fight about are: sex, money, children, household duties, communication, time, jealousy, relatives, just to name a few. But haven't you ever had a fight and made up with your partner, only to find within a short time you're fighting all over again? Or haven't you ever fought about one issue one week, and the next week, that same issue didn't even bother you? Here's the explanation for this frustrating pattern:

You're never fighting for the reason you think you're fighting. You're fighting for one of two reasons:

1. **You aren't receiving the love, support, appreciation, or understanding you need from your partner, and emotional separation has built up between you.**

2. **Old repressed feelings are surfacing and magnifying the present situation into something more upsetting than it actually is.**

Most conflict on the surface of a relationship comes from a much deeper place within the relationship, a place where you store "emotional tension." Emotional tension is a state of emotional un-ease or lack of balance. When you're a child, any unresolved hurtful experiences get stored in your subconscious as emotional tension. (See Question 12.) In your adulthood, that emotional tension increases whenever you don't feel loved, appreciated, or understood, especially by your intimate partner. Imagine a big pressure cooker inside of you, and one inside your partner. Each time one or both of you gets triggered by something that happens or something the other says, it sets off that pressure cooker of anger and you get into a fight.

For instance, maybe you've been feeling neglected by your wife for months, and are unconsciously angry at her for ignoring you. Instead of acknowledging and communicating about the emotional tension that's built up, you find yourself becoming really upset with her for arriving home ten minutes later than she promised. You end up in a big argument, but the problem is, you aren't arguing about the real issue: your feelings of neglect. You're arguing about her late arrival. Therefore, even if you come to some sense of resolution, you haven't dealt with the true source of the conflict, and guess what—it's going to find another way to express itself again in an hour, or a day, or next week. This explains why you and your partner seem to be fighting all the time about the same issues, even after you've made some agreements. *You're not fighting about the right issues!!!*

Sit down together as a couple and discuss this principle of stored up emotional tension as the cause for constant fighting. Hopefully, you will both commit to doing some intensive work on your relationship by first, becoming familiar with the emotional baggage you've carried into your marriage, and secondly, communicating about and healing those old unresolved emotions from the past so they don't keep spilling over into the present and sabotaging your love. Next, you need to do some emotional housecleaning on your marriage. Take an honest look at the needs that aren't being fulfilled by your partner; ask yourself if you're feeling loved and appreciated enough; uncover any hidden resentments that have been lurking beneath the surface. When you and your mate work together in this way as a team, you'll find yourselves fighting a lot less, and loving a lot more!!!

►❤❤❤► *SEE ALSO QUESTION 12*

*Whenever my husband and I fight, he doesn't just get an-
gry—he gets mean. He calls me awful names, insults me,
and acts like an attack dog. We always make up eventually,
but after four years of marriage, I'm starting to feel beaten
down. When I try to talk to him about this, he gets defensive and accuses me of being too sensitive. What should I
do?*

━━❤❤❤━━▶ You say that your husband becomes
mean whenever you fight. If that's the only time this
behavior arises, it probably means you're dealing
with a man who, believe it or not, is scared to death
of anger. I'll bet you anything that your husband felt
somehow controlled, overpowered, or manipulated
by one of his parents or siblings as a child, especially
during fights. Maybe he had an abusive parent.
Maybe his big brother was a bully. *According to his
emotional programming (see Question 12), he unconsciously decided that, as an adult, whenever he feels at-
tacked, or perceives some kind of threat, he should go on the
offensive, like an animal who barks wildly defending his
territory, hoping to scare the intruder away.* Funny, you
called him an attack dog, didn't you . . . !?

Whenever you criticize your husband, or express any feelings of discontent about your marriage, he perceives you as "the enemy" and tries to
hurt you to defend himself. No wonder you feel

beaten down. It's essential that he understand two things:

1. **His verbally abusive behavior during fighting must stop.** You may need to give him an ultimatum stating that it isn't acceptable for him to name-call and put you down during arguments, and that, when he feels that rage, he needs to take time-outs in order to separate his genuine upset with you from his old, stored-up anger, and then resume the conversation. He might even want to go into another room and hit a pillow until he begins to get in touch with the grief and hurt under that rage, so he can release those old feelings that are trying to be released for the purpose of healing. (See Question 38.) *Let him know that although you support him in cleaning out all his old anger, he can't just dump those feelings on you.*

2. **He needs to get some professional help in understanding and healing his old rage.** Your husband probably hates himself at those times when he lashes out at you, but doesn't know how to do it any differently. Insist that he find a qualified professional who can educate him in anger management and facilitate his doing some emotional work to locate the true source of the anger. It will also be good for

you both, at some point, to have some sessions together where you learn healthy fighting skills.

These are not suggestions—they are absolute
commitments you need from him in order for the relationship to continue. Verbal abuse is, in many
ways, more insidious than physical abuse, because
it's easier to ignore and excuse. But don't kid yourself, it's just as deadly.

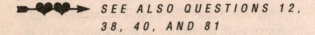 *SEE ALSO QUESTIONS 12,
38, 40, AND 81*

How do I deal with a partner who is physically abusive?

My husband has a bad temper, and sometimes when we argue, he pushes me or hits me. This doesn't happen often, and he always cries afterwards and tells me he's sorry. I know he came from a very abusive home and was beaten by his father. I love him very much and am trying to be understanding, but these incidents are making it hard for me to trust him. I'm also worried about the effect they will have on our young children. How can I help him and get him to stop?

━♥♥➤ *Don't help him. Help yourself and get out now!!* I don't care if he was abused as a child, or how many times he apologizes. You are married to a batterer and you are typically codependent in making excuses for him, rather than thinking about your own welfare. It is never acceptable under any circumstances for someone to use physical violence against another person. Yes, your husband has a serious problem and needs help, but so do you, because you are in major denial about what's been going on. This isn't a "bad temper"—it's physical abuse. And it's a little late to worry about the effect on your children. Believe me, they're already damaged enough by what has gone on so far.

Before you talk yourself out of it, before you get advice from everyone you know, you need to physically separate from him. **Either insist that he leave,** or take the children and leave yourself. Let him know that if he wants the marriage to continue, he needs to seek immediate and intensive professional help. There are therapists who deal specifically with male batterers, as well as special support groups he will probably have to attend. *This is not an option—it must be a prerequisite for any type of reconciliation.* He must make progress emotionally and behaviorally before you live together again.

At the same time, you need to seek help for yourself. As a victim, you are just as enmeshed as he is in the pattern of violence. You have your own unresolved childhood issues that attracted you to this kind of person (see Question 15), and must heal your own lack of self-esteem. Your children will also need some professional help with their emotions—they were battered too, just by being in that environment.

Every community has a Battered Women's Hot Line where counselors are available to support you in making the decision to leave, and to ensure your safety. Don't hesitate to call if you feel you can't do this on your own. And remember—you need to break the cycle now, before it's too late, for yourself and for your children.

➤ ❤❤❤ ➤ *SEE ALSO QUESTION 15*

44 *What does it mean if a couple never fights? Can this hurt a relationship?*

Sometimes I wonder if something is wrong with my marriage, because my mate and I never fight, or even have a disagreement. We both came from very strict, religious homes and never saw our parents argue either. We get along well, but you wouldn't call our relationship very passionate. It's more calm and careful. Are we missing something?

➤♥♥➤ Yes—it's called honesty! No matter how compatible you and your mate are, you are still two different and unique human beings. For that reason, it is inevitable that you wouldn't see eye to eye about everything for every day of your life together—unless, that is, you tiptoe around each other, fearful of rocking the boat, and that's exactly what you're doing. *Couples who never even disagree are engaged in what I call "careful loving."* One or both partners fear that conflict of any kind would be dangerous to the relationship, so they avoid it at all costs. The result? A consistent and boring marriage.

You said it yourself; your relationship isn't passionate. That's because, as I discussed earlier in describing the Emotional Map (see Question 38), *when you suppress all of the unpleasant emotions, such as anger, irritation, hurt, or sadness, you end up cutting yourself off from the love and passion as well.* You feel "I love my partner, but I don't feel 'in love' anymore." You're killing your passion with kindness. **Even though the issues you pretend don't exist between you may not be that significant in themselves, it is your decision to ignore them that *is* significant, because in numbing yourself to your pain, you rob yourself of the ability to feel great joy.**

You already suspect that both you and your mate made some pretty strong, unconscious, and unhealthy decisions when you were growing up about how unsafe you felt communicating any unpleasant feelings. *Children from very strict or dogmatic religious homes often aren't given permission to feel or express "unholy" emotions. They may even be taught that feeling emotions like anger, resentment, or even fear is sinful, or a sign of lack of faith.* So your partner does something that upsets you, but you unconsciously and automatically suppress that feeling, not even allowing yourself to recognize its existence. When this pattern of suppression occurs enough times, you end up in a marriage that lacks vitality, honesty, and a passionate connection between the two of you.

The good news is that both you and your partner seem ready to make a change. Make a new commitment to building a relationship based on complete communication of all your feelings. Read, take classes, and do everything you can to educate yourself about how to have a dynamic and intimate relationship. *Trust in your marriage enough to know that it will not only withstand disagreements and even arguments, but that it will grow stronger each time you transcend a conflict and return to love.*

►—❤❤❤—► *SEE ALSO QUESTIONS 37 AND 38*

45 *How can I ask my partner for what I need without sounding like I'm being too demanding?*

Whenever I try to express my needs to my partner, he accuses me of being "demanding." I try to be careful about how I ask for what I want, but no matter what I do, he gets defensive and won't listen. Is there a way I can ask for the things I need without making him feel I'm trying to control him?

—❤❤❤— There are two possibilities here. The first is that your partner is a very emotionally wounded individual who has a really serious problem giving love without feeling he is losing something in the process. Maybe he spent his childhood always giving and never receiving. Maybe he had a mother who leaned on him for the love, affection, and support she should have gotten from her husband, and used him as a surrogate. This would result in his despising women who appear "needy," and therefore, no matter what you say, or how you explain your feelings, he will always feel you are too "demanding." *For this type of man, the perfect relationship is one in which the woman asks for nothing and gratefully accepts whatever she can get from him, whenever he wants to give it.* In other words, he's looking for a doormat, not a woman.

If you suspect this is the case, end this relationship now if you don't want to lose all of your self-esteem and feel like an emotional beggar. Then, ask yourself why you were attracted to someone who made you feel your needs aren't okay. Who does this man represent? Your father, who wasn't there for you? Your mother, who was so busy with other kids or work or an addiction that your needs weren't important? Do some work on understanding and healing your emotional programming (see Questions 12 and 15).

Now for the second possibility. Maybe your boyfriend is an otherwise wonderful guy, and it's only when you directly ask him for something that he reacts defensively. In this case, you're experiencing a common male/female dynamic based on a psychological difference between the sexes. Here's the key: **your boyfriend is interpreting your expression of your needs and desires as criticisms of his performance in the relationship.**

Here's a quick lesson in male psychology from my book *Secrets About Men Every Woman Should Know*. From their earliest upbringing, and for thousands of years, men have been trained to feel that their role is to master the outer world of action and accomplishment, rather than the inner world of thought and feeling. More often than not, little boys are taught that their value is in what they do and the things they achieve. Even with very conscious parents who attempt to avoid gender bias, boys model themselves after fathers and grandfathers who were programmed more traditionally. **So, based on this, little boys conclude that "in order to be good, I have to do it right," and they equate their self-esteem with accomplishment.**

When a woman appears to challenge a man's ability to do anything perfectly, he may react defensively, because he interprets her feedback as if she is saying "You did it wrong. You're not making me happy. Therefore, you are a bad boy." Often, he may not even hear the details of her request for a change in behavior, or remember her suggestions. *After initially determining that she doesn't think he is doing something perfectly, his emotional reflexes take over, and he switches into defensive mode.*

Here's how it works in your relationship. You say to your partner, "I need more verbal affection from you. I know you love me, but I'd like to hear it more often." You figure that an appropriate response would be something like "I'll try," or "It's hard for me to express my feelings, but I want you to know how much I do love you." Instead, he becomes instantly defensive and counterattacks by calling you "demanding." What's happening? *Possibly, he interprets your request as a statement like "You are not being a good boyfriend. You aren't making me happy. You are a failure."* And if he was criticized as a child, he may also have an "emotional flashback" in that moment with you, and reexperience some of the anger and pain he felt as a little boy being told he wasn't good enough. All that anger gets turned back on poor, unsuspecting you. Sound familiar?

If you're sure your boyfriend isn't the abusive person described in the first part of this answer, read him this section of the book, and ask him what he thinks about all I've said. Hopefully, he'll relate to my description of what goes on inside him, and you'll both gain insight into this frustrating dynamic. Let him know you don't want to make him wrong, and that you want to work together with him so you can give him feedback without his feeling you are criticizing him. You might also read Question 31 and do the exercise I suggested.

As for what you can do on your own, I have several suggestions. First, avoid using language that makes him feel wrong when you are asking for what you want. For instance, **don't say: "You never tell me I'm pretty, or notice my clothes. Why don't you pay more attention to me? This always happens." In-stead, say: "Honey, whenever you notice what I'm wearing, it makes me feel so special. I know it may seem unimportant to you, but if you compliment me when I get dressed up, it would really make me happy. I need to know you like how I look."** And second, make sure you're giving your boyfriend enough positive messages about the things you are happy with in the relationship, so he gains a sense of confidence and self-esteem. Then, when you ask for something, he may feel safer in opening up and giving it to you.

➤❤❤➤   *SEE ALSO QUESTIONS 12,
              15, 31, 36, AND 37*

46

How do you handle a partner who is very critical of you?

My girlfriend keeps trying to change everything about me, from how I dress, what I read, the grammar I use when I speak, even who my friends are. Nothing I do is ever perfect enough, and I live with constant criticism. I'm afraid I'll never live up to her expectations. How can I get her to be less critical?

➤ ❤❤❤ ➤   You are asking the wrong question. *Instead of asking me "How can I get her to be less critical?" you should be asking yourself "Why am I punishing myself by being in a relationship with someone who treats me like dirt?"* Your girlfriend is making herself very clear—she doesn't like you very much! She obviously sees you as someone whom she can either emotionally torture or rehabilitate, depending on the mood she's in. You're right . . . you can never live up to her expectations, because she is expecting you to be someone you aren't. **This isn't a relationship—it's self-flagellation on your part!**

So what's the answer to the real question: Why would you be attracted to a woman who treats you so terribly? You know what I'm going to say—it goes back to your emotional programming from childhood (see Questions 12 and 15). *You're undoubtedly repeating a pattern you first experienced when you were young, one in which you had to work hard to gain the attention, praise, or approval of someone whom you loved very much.* Maybe Dad or Mom was super critical, and nothing you did was ever good enough. Your grades should have been better, you should have excelled more at sports, you should have had a better attitude, etc. etc. You may have made an unconscious decision that "I'm not good enough, and I have to work hard to get someone to love me." **By attracting a woman who treats you like a child she's trying to "raise" properly, you've put yourself right back home with your parents. It's as if you are trying to finish that unfinished emotional business— "maybe this time, I'll finally please someone I love."**

Maybe it wasn't you who was criticized as a child, but one of your parents by the other. Perhaps Mom tongue-lashed Dad constantly, and he was a lovable but pathetic wimp. In trying to unconsciously be loyal to Dad, you choose women like his wife, and tolerate the same abuse he did. *We often act out one parent's role with the other in a psychological attempt to "keep that parent company" in his pain.* **I've seen people who are doing this find it extremely difficult to break their family pattern, feeling almost as if leaving an unhealthy or abusive situation similar to their parent's would be a kind of betrayal of that parent.**

No matter what your reason for being involved with a woman who treats you in this demeaning fashion, one thing is clear: You need to end the rela-

tionship now! I suggest taking some time off from relationships for a while, so you can do some emotional
healing and fill yourself up from the inside out. *When
you're loving yourself more, you'll be less inclined to attract partners who don't know how to love you.*

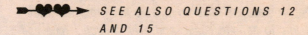 **SEE ALSO QUESTIONS 12
AND 15**

47

Is there a way to detect symptoms of trouble in your relationship so you can solve the problems before they get too serious?

I'm married for the second time, and I find myself worrying that, one day, the relationship will explode in my face. I know this fear comes from the way my first marriage ended. I thought everything was fine, until my husband came to me, told me he was very unhappy and that he was leaving. I fell apart, because I had no idea we had problems. I don't want this to happen again, and even though I hate confrontation, I don't want to live in a dream world this time. Is there some way to tell if problems exist before they ruin the relationship?

➤━♥♥♥━➤ You're right—relationships don't just fall apart overnight. There are warning signs to look for that the relationship is in trouble, and the sooner you spot these, the better your chances for resolving the problems and making the marriage even stronger. One easy way to spot danger is called **"The Four R's."**

The Four R's are the four stages of the deterioration of intimacy, four increasing stages of tension that build up between you and your partner. The Four R's are four words that begin with the letter R: *Resistance, Resentment, Rejection, and Repression.* Let's go through each one and, if you're in a relationship right now that has some problems, you can follow along and see what stage you're in. Or you can think about your past relationship that you're no longer in and see how it went right through those Four R's.

The first "R" is Resistance. It is the first stage of tension building up. And it's natural for this stage to come and go in an intimate relationship from time to time. Resistances are those little things that bother you about somebody, those little annoyances. He leaves the towels on the floor, she talks on the phone too much. Yesterday he said something to hurt your feelings. These aren't life-shattering issues, but the problem lies in the way most of us handle little resistances: **we ignore them and pretend nothing is wrong.** You tell yourself things like, "Don't get so upset over nothing," or "You're being too picky," or "Let's not rock the boat." And when you don't resolve those feelings of resistance by talking about them, you push them down. More resistances appear, and you push those down too, until they build up and up. One day suddenly you're feeling Resentment and you're in the second R.

Resentment is when there are so many little resistances that build up, they create a feeling of resentment. Now you're not just annoyed, you're angry. Now it's not just "I wish he wouldn't tell that stupid story at every party we go to." Now it's, "I hate that story. If I hear that story one more time, I'm going to scream!" See the difference? **You know you're in Resentment when you're starting to feel angry, frustrated, a lit-**

tle more unloving, a little more distant from your
partner. You're not feeling this resentment twenty-
four hours a day every day, but there are more moments in the relationship when you're feeling less
closeness and intimacy with your mate. You're also
finding yourself being more critical, even if you simply think those criticisms to yourself.

One of the biggest signs that you're in Stage
Two, Resentment, is that your sex life is starting to
change. *See, you cannot be attracted to someone at
whom you feel growing anger. Anger kills passion.*
You'll notice that you're a little turned off, a little less
interested in sex. If you don't deal with the feelings of
resentment building up in the relationship and resolve them, the resentment builds up and builds up
and turns into the third R, Rejection.

*Rejection means separation; it means that there is a
wall between you, and emotionally you are not connected
in the same way. You may still be living together, but you
have separated your hearts from one another.* So much resistance, so much tension has built up that it's impossible for you to stay emotionally close to the other
person. So you pull away. You may do this by fighting or criticizing your partner a lot, finding yourself
attracted to other people, fantasizing about leaving,
or just leading a very separate life from your mate.
Some couples in this third stage hardly see one another, but still deny that anything's wrong. Others
are more dramatic in their rejection, threatening to

leave, and escalating the emotional and verbal hurt and abuse in the relationship.

Of course in this stage of Rejection, it is very hard to have any kind of sex life, because there is too much tension between you. You may simply feel a lack of attraction, and tell yourself it's because of the kids, or because you're busy. But the truth is, the sexual chemistry is buried underneath piles of Resistances and Resentments.

Many relationships don't survive this stage. However, if you don't separate, and continue letting all those feelings of rejection build up, you will eventually enter the final stage of the Four R's, Repression. **Repression is the state of emotional numbness. You enter into this stage when you're just so tired of resisting and resenting and rejecting that you successfully repress all your negative emotions, numbing yourself in order to be comfortable.** You tell yourself "You know, things aren't that bad," or "We're too old to experience romance, anyway," or "We have to stay together for the sake of the children." Your life goes on, but with no passion. By repressing the tension, you've also successfully repressed your joy.

Repression is the most dangerous of the Four R's, because in this stage, you can fool yourself into believing that everything is "fine." I often see couples who are obviously having problems, but deny that there's a problem at all. "Everything's fine, we've worked it all out," they insist. Of course they probably have little, if any, sex life anymore. A couple in stage four might *appear* to be content; they may never argue; they may behave very politely toward one another. You may even envy their relationship, until one day you hear that they separated or got divorced, and you think, "I can't understand it, they always seemed so happy." "Seemed" is the right choice of words. They repressed all their unpleasant emotions, and ended up killing the relationship.

So be on the lookout for the Four R's. *As soon as you notice a little tension building up, communicate about your feelings with your partner, preferably using the Emotional Map.* (See Question 38.) It's a lot easier to resolve a small conflict than a big one that's been brewing for a long time. Don't wait! Don't overlook issues that seem "too small." Even if your relationship is in an advanced stage of the Four R's, it is possible to find your way back to love again. How? By acknowledging all that emotional tension, communicating about it, and healing the resentments that created the walls between you.

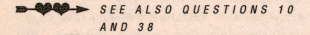 **SEE ALSO QUESTIONS 10 AND 38**

48

Is it possible to have a good marriage when your partner is a control freak?

I am married to the biggest control freak of all time, and it's causing tremendous tension in our relationship. My husband always has to have everything his way, from the route we take driving somewhere, to how the dishes are placed in the dishwasher, to when we have sex. When I met him, I was attracted to his strong personality, because my last boyfriend was a wimp, but I didn't realize that for my husband, strong means that I have to be weak. We are in a constant power struggle, unless I just give in. Can our marriage work?

➤❤❤❤➤ Sure your marriage can work, if you don't mind being a submissive, powerless slave with no freedom to be yourself. I'll bet your husband thinks your relationship's working just fine, and why shouldn't he? You do what he tells you to do, and he remains unchallenged. *When a person is married to a control freak (and you most certainly are!), the dynamic of the relationship is about who wins and who loses, and not about love.* As long as your husband feels he is winning every interaction, he will be happy, because that is his true agenda—not to be a caring husband who pleases you, but to validate his own illusion of omnipotence over and over again.

Most human beings like to feel in control of their lives, and feel uncomfortable being out of control. The difference is that **control freaks *must* be in con-**

trol of their lives, and *will do anything to avoid feeling out of control.* This presents serious problems in relationships:

- *Control freaks have a difficult time opening up* and showing you their vulnerable and emotional side.
- *Control freaks don't like to admit that they need you,* OR . . .
- *Control freaks need you so much they* want to control all of your time, becoming highly possessive and jealous.
- *Control freaks can become easily upset,* expressing either anger or hurt, when they don't get their way or feel out of control.
- *Control freaks can be compulsive* about their living habits, routine, work, etc., and therefore, very difficult to live with.
- *Control freaks can attempt to control the choices and habits of those around them*—coworkers, friends, children, and YOU!
- *Control freaks don't ever like being told what to do*—it makes them feel out of control.
- *Control freaks may have sexual problems*—either a difficult time letting go in bed, an attachment to a particular idea of how sex "should" be, a need to control you but a resistance to losing control himself.
- *Control freaks have a hard time relaxing,* whether

after work, on weekends, or on vacations; they may be workaholics.

- *Control freaks can be very impatient and irritable.*
- *Control freaks may become very domineering and critical parents,* since by definition, babies and young children are out of control, and therefore drive control freaks crazy.

Sounds really enticing, doesn't it? As you already know, living with a control freak is anything but enjoyable—in fact, it's pure hell. As for your husband, like most control freaks, in his childhood he probably felt controlled by adults or circumstances that rendered him powerless. At some point, he made an unconscious decision that, when he grew up, he'd never be out of control again. And he will stick to that decision, because to him it feels like a matter of life and death. *That's why this is one of the most difficult kinds of emotional damage to heal (see Question 12), since by definition, a control freak hates being out of control, and that includes admitting he has a problem, or giving in to an ultimatum by a partner.*

As for you, you fit the description of a classic victim who mistakes her partner's addiction for power, who is looking for someone to take charge of her life, and who associates love with control (see Question 15). Can't you feel yourself slowly dying? It's time to break free of the emotional prison you've placed yourself in. *Get whatever help and support you need to leave your husband now.* Even if, by some miracle, he were to agree to seek help and eventually underwent an amazing transformation, you would still need physical and emotional space between you to break the old cycle and reclaim your self before giving the relationship another chance. **Remember: love that is healthy will always empower you, not imprison you.**

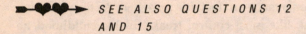 *SEE ALSO QUESTIONS 12 AND 15*

49

Should you tell your mate bad things from your past even if you're afraid it will hurt the relationship?

I have a terrible, dark secret that I've kept from my husband for seven years, because I'm too ashamed to tell him. My secret is that I was sexually abused by my stepfather from the age of six to fourteen. I met my husband when I was seventeen, and we got married right out of high school. We have a good marriage, but I suspect that a lot of my problems, particularly in bed, stem from the abuse. I'm terrified that my husband will hate me for lying to him all these years, or worse, will think I'm a bad, dirty person. Do I need to tell him about my past? If I don't, will it hurt our marriage?

There is an old saying, *"We are only as sick as the secrets we keep."* You have been carrying this secret inside your heart all your life, and the shame you feel is, as you suspect, hurting your ability to give and receive love in your marriage. *A long-term sexually abusive relationship creates an enormous emotional wound in a person, not only because of the sexual violation, but because of the fear, powerlessness, loss of control, and guilt you experienced.* You may have been told by your stepfather that you were a bad girl, or that people would believe you were bad if they knew what you'd done. And his voice is still in your head, preventing you from reaching out to your husband for the unconditional love and acceptance you so desperately need. (See Question 60.)

You are not bad. You are not dirty. You are a victim of a deeply disturbed man who violated you sexually, emotionally, and spiritually. He thought he won, but in fact, he lost, because you went on to marry a good person who loves you deeply. I'm proud of you—you transcended enough of your shame to feel you deserved a wonderful husband, and you found him! Believe me, that's much more happiness than many victims of sexual abuse allow themselves to have. *Now, you're ready for your next step—to trust your husband enough to know he will love you in spite of your past.*

I know it's very frightening to think of letting your husband into that dark room inside your heart. **But I'll bet you anything that he knows it's there, and has been trying to get in so that he can help free you from your emotional prison. In fact, you will probably be surprised to see how relieved he is when you tell him the cause of your pain and that it has nothing to do with him.** He's probably been worrying that you don't love him as much as he loves you, or are somehow turned off by him. Once he understands what you've been going through, he can offer you the support and strength you need to conquer this demon. And herein lies the key to your true healing—trusting a man who doesn't betray you and who won't let you down will allow that part of you to open up again. *The truth will set you free.*

➤❤❤❤➤ *SEE ALSO QUESTION 60*

50

Shouldn't my partner understand how I want him to love me without my having to explain it all the time?

My boyfriend and I have this ongoing disagreement about our relationship. I feel that if he really loves me, he should know how to make me happy, and I shouldn't have to explain every little thing I need to him. He insists that he can't "read my mind," and wants me to spell it all out in detail. This seems so unromantic to me. I feel like he's just being lazy. What do you think?

➤❤❤❤➤ I don't think your boyfriend is being lazy—I think he's being honest. In fact, I hear this same complaint, mostly from men, all the time: *"My wife expects me to be a mind reader. She acts like there are these mysterious things I'm supposed to know about what she wants and needs, and then gets mad at me for not figuring them out. How am I supposed to know what she wants?"* That's a good question—how do you expect your husband to know your innermost desires? After all, he's not a woman, so he won't naturally understand you like other women will. And if he's been with women before you, each one has been different and unique. You are the first "you" he's ever loved!!!

Like many women, you've fallen prey to what I call one of the most common "Love Myths"—false notions about love that can actually hurt a relationship. The Love Myth I'm referring to is: **"If my partner really loves me, he will know just what I need."**

You won't ever have to ask him for anything; you won't have to tell him your secret fantasies. If he is the "right one," he will automatically know your innermost thoughts and feelings. Doesn't this sound like a fairy tale or romantic movie? Well guess what? That's where you and tens of millions of other women probably got the idea that your true lover won't need you to educate him about you—he'll just "know" you. *You form this picture of your ideal lover when you are still a young girl, and by time you meet your flesh-and-blood prince charming, he has all sorts of unconscious expectations to live up to.*

Here's the problem: **when you expect your lover to automatically know how to please you, you are setting him up for failure.** He will feel like you are testing him (which you are!), manipulating him, and trying to control him by making him "guess" what you want, rather than coming out and telling him. *When a man feels these silent expectations placed upon him, he will often respond with rebelliousness.* Even if he wanted to please you before, now he's too angry to care! You think he's being lazy, or uncooperative, or resistant when he asks you to spell out what it is that you want, when, in truth, he's just being practical.

All I'm suggesting is that you try educating your husband about your needs and your preferences, from how you like to be treated on your birthday to how you like to be touched in bed. Maybe this doesn't fit your romantic fantasy picture, but it's a lot more realistic, and will end up bringing you much more fulfillment. Believe me, there are a lot of unhappy and unloved women out there who would be thrilled to have their husband even ask "How can I make you happy?" They wouldn't think of responding by saying, "Guess . . ." They'd give him a three-page typewritten list!!

So instead of believing the myth "If my husband really loves me, he will know just how to please me," adopt a new, more healthy belief: "If my husband really loves me, he will *ask me* just how he can please me!" Your husband already did ask, so consider yourself one very lucky wife.

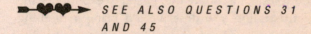 *SEE ALSO QUESTIONS 31 AND 45*

51 *Why do men hate talking about emotional issues late at night?*

My husband and I have been married for ten years, and consider ourselves very happy, but we butt heads over this one issue all the time: whenever I want to talk about our relationship or a problem we're having, and it's late at night, he shuts down and refuses to discuss anything. All I'm trying to do is work on our marriage, but he accuses me of trying to ruin his sleep by deliberately waiting until we're in bed to bring up disturbing topics. I feel like he's just making excuses so he can avoid dealing with my complaints. What's the solution?

▬❤❤❤▬▶ Boy, can millions of women relate to your question, including me! I used to experience the same frustration you describe: I'd bring something up to my husband in bed, and he'd either pretend to listen, but fall asleep during the conversation, or get angry with me for trying to control, and make comments like "Why do we always have to talk about things when *you* want to?" Finally, while I was doing my research for *Secrets About Men Every Woman Should Know*, I took the time to really examine this dynamic, and figured out the following:

1. *Men feel less in control late at night when they are tired, and so feel less secure having an important conversation.* Often men instinctively look at a delicate conversation with their wives as a

potential power struggle. When the conversation is emotional in content, men already feel at a disadvantage, since most women are more comfortable identifying and discussing feelings. So your partner might try to postpone having a discussion when he's feeling fatigued, because he knows he isn't going to be able to feel in control as much as he'd like to. And since men need to concentrate in order to be emotionally articulate, your husband knows he won't be at his best just before bed. (Perhaps this is why women secretly like talking to men when they're tired, because we know their resistance is lower and their mind isn't as sharp!!)

2. *Men fear you will go on and on and they won't get any sleep.* When it's late at night, and you want to have a serious talk, your man knows he is a captive audience, and a fear rises up within him: **"She'll start talking and never stop! We'll be up all night. I'll be exhausted for work tomorrow, and I'll make mistakes on the job. I'll get fired. I'll be a failure. Well, that settles it, no way she's tricking me into having a discussion tonight!"**

Now, let's admit the truth, ladies: He's at least partially right! We *will* go on and on if we don't think he's getting our point, even if it keeps us up for hours! This is a mistake in itself, since men often need time to "mull" over what we've said before they can respond. *I've learned that a little patience goes a long way in helping your partner feel safe talking about issues without worrying that you will be relentless, and pressure him into responding immediately.*

Here's what I suggest: Share this information with your husband, and see if he can relate to all I've said. Then, make some agreements about late-night discussion. Perhaps he'll ask you to bring issues up earlier in the evening. Perhaps you'll respond by saying he is usually busy reading the paper or watching TV, and you will have to both compromise and learn to make time for communicating when it works for each of you. As for those urges to talk in bed, here's what I do: I say to my husband, *"Honey, I need to talk with you about something that I realized upset me today, or something that has been on my mind, and I'll need about fifteen minutes. I know you're tired, but I'll feel better if I can just get it off my chest before we go to sleep. How does this sound to you? If you'd rather make an appointment to discuss it tomorrow, let me know."*

Now my husband has two options, and men like options—he can give me the fifteen minutes so I at least make a dent in my feelings and he can show me he does care; or, if he is really exhausted and not receptive, he can (lovingly!) tell me that he certainly wants to hear what I have to say, but that he's in no shape to listen, and suggest a time the next day for our discussion. Obviously, if he keeps postponing our talk, and never finds time, that's an entirely different issue. However, I think you'll find him very appreciative of the information I've shared with you, and you'll avoid those nasty late-night arguments.

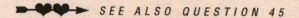 *SEE ALSO QUESTION 45*

Sex and
Physical Affection

How can I get my partner to give me more physical affection when we're not having sex?

The only time my husband touches me is when he wants sex. I'm a very affectionate person, and feel frustrated with him. How can I explain to him that I need more physical affection in general, hugging, hand-holding, cuddling, and not just sex?

►❤❤❤► To your husband, and to all men of the world, listen for a few moments to what your women have been trying to tell you: *We love you, and want to connect with you physically as much as possible, but please don't wait to touch us until you want to have sex!* When you do, we will not be ready to receive you with the passion and acceptance you deserve. **A woman's heart needs to be full before her body can overflow with desire for you.** Each time you take our hand, stroke our hair, reach out for a hug, or plant a light kiss on our lips for no reason at all, it is as if you are saying "I love you." We literally feel our hearts fill with joy and contentment. That is just the way we are designed. We understand that it is different for you, and need you to understand that it is different for us.

Think of it as building a fire. You light the kindling, and slowly, at the right moment, place each new log onto the flames, allowing the embers to become hot and glowing, until eventually, the fire is blazing. This is how it is for our bodies. Each caress,

*each embrace kindles the fire of desire within our
bodies, and our passion slowly builds until we burn
with longing for you. You wouldn't expect a fire to be
burning strongly after just striking a match and
placing a fresh log upon it. In this same way, know
that you cannot expect us to be "ready" on Saturday
night if you have not even touched us or loved us all
week long.*

This is what transforms mere sex into true lovemaking. *Making love is not just about sex—it is about
making those real moments of love with your beloved.* If
you limit your lovemaking to your sexual time together, you are ripping yourself off. It will help to
stop thinking that lovemaking begins in the bedroom. The bedroom may be a comfortable place to
have sex, but if you wait until you get there to begin
making love, you'll be too late, and we, as your
women, will probably have a difficult time catching
up with you.

This isn't just about what creates more passion
in women, by the way. You too, men, can learn to
build your own fire of love, attraction, and desire by
allowing yourself more moments of physical affection with your partner outside of a purely sexual context. Don't fall into the trap of what I call the *"All or
Nothing Syndrome."* **This is the belief that tells a man
he can't get turned on unless he goes "all the way,"
so he avoids doing anything (kissing his wife, cuddling in the morning) that might arouse him, since**

he may not have time to "do anything"—meaning, of course, have intercourse. Many men unconsciously tell themselves "Look, we don't have time to really get into this, so why even hold her and kiss her!"

Men, don't be in such a hurry to get rid of any little feeling of love or sexual energy by ejaculating as soon as possible! *Allow that energy to build up in your body and learn to pull it up into your heart.* You'll find your love for your partner expanding, your desire deepening, and when you do finally make love, you'll experience new levels of joy and ecstasy you hadn't even imagined were possible.

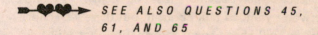 *SEE ALSO QUESTIONS 45, 61, AND 65*

53 How can I get my partner to initiate sex more, instead of waiting for me to always be the one who wants it?

In my relationship with my wife, I'm always the one who initiates sex. If I don't make an overture, we won't make love. I've asked her to be more sexually aggressive, but nothing changes. I feel like she'd be happy if we never had sex. I'm tired of always making the moves. How can I get her to be the initiator?

➡❤❤❤➤ You already know that you can't "get" your wife to be the initiator. The question is, why doesn't she initiate sexual activity with you? This may sound silly, but have you tried asking her, *"Honey, why don't you initiate sex more often?"* Perhaps she won't want to talk about it, but there's a chance that she will share some information that will help you understand what's going on inside her.

In case she doesn't wish to volunteer that information, let me explain some of the reasons why women might seem disinterested in or don't initiate sex:

1. *She was taught that "good girls aren't supposed to show that they enjoy sex."*

In our sexually repressed society, women are frequently brought up to believe that girls who like sex are loose, sleazy, and not the kind that men want to marry. We often unconsciously or consciously learn to suppress our sensuality and sexuality, fearing what will happen to us if we let it out. *Your wife may have received strong messages to this effect from her parents or her church, and therefore, finds it difficult to initiate sex because that makes it look like she likes sex, and consequently, is bad or dirty.*

You didn't mention whether or not your wife enjoys sex when you initiate it. If she does, I'd say the above reason is probably the cause of her lack of sexual aggression. Talk to her about the sexual messages she received as a child. Explain how pressured you feel always being the one who is the aggressor; after all, it's an emotional risk to approach someone you love and let them know you want to be intimate, since you are setting yourself up for possible rejection. Tell her how loved and wanted you feel when she shows you she wants *you*, and reassure her that this makes you respect her even more.

   2. *She likes sex, but may not be turned on by you or enjoy the way you make love to her.*

I can't tell you how many times a husband will complain to me that his wife doesn't like sex, but when I speak to her in private, she confesses that *it's not sex she doesn't like, but sex with him!* She just doesn't like the way he makes love to her. I know this might be very painful to consider, but if you're a man whose wife is avoiding sex, or won't initiate sex, find the courage to ask her: **"Would you enjoy sex more if I made love to you differently?"** If her answer is "Yes!" put your ego aside, and be open to hearing her sexual likes and dislikes, the needs you may not be fulfilling, and her fantasy about how she would like you to make love to her. This may be difficult to discuss without professional help, so find a qualified sex therapist or counselor if you need help in communicating more honestly and openly about sex.

3. *She may not like sex due to some emotional trauma.*

If you discuss these issues with your wife, and she claims she just doesn't care about sex, don't accept this at face value. Asexuality is more complex than it appears. I don't believe there is such a thing as a person simply "not liking sex." **A disinterest in sex usually covers up an aversion to sex.** This can stem from fear of intimacy, fear of being controlled, suppressed anger (hers at you), but *if the sexual disinterest has been a lifelong problem, it can usually be traced to serious emotional trauma such as sexual molestation, rape, incest, or other violent forms of abuse.* Your wife may not even be aware of the connection between her emotional wounds and her aversion to sex. In fact, she may not even remember the events that could have programmed her to avoid sexual contact. If you suspect that she is a victim of this kind of trauma, do everything in your power to get her some professional help, not just for the sake of your marriage, but for the sake of her own mental peace.

54

Is it okay to have sexual fantasies about someone else when you're making love to your own partner?

My husband and I have an ongoing fight about something that really bothers me. He often fantasizes about other women when we're making love and insists that there's nothing wrong with it. I feel really hurt and rejected when I think of him doing this, and want him to stop. Who's right?

➡️💕💕➡️ *First of all, let's get something straight—if your husband is in bed with you, but fantasizing about someone else, he's not making love to you: he's screwing you, and making love to her!!* Of course you feel rejected and betrayed when your husband is having sex with you and thinking about someone else. *He's cheating on you mentally!* How does he expect you to feel . . . overjoyed? Is he so narcissistic, childish, and self-indulgent that he actually wants to hear you say *"Oh honey, it's perfectly fine that you're lying here lusting after some other woman's body, getting turned on by the thought of touching her, while you use me as a receptacle for your semen! Go right ahead. Don't mind me. In fact, why not put a bag over my head so you don't get distracted from your fantasy?"*

Now I know that many so-called respected psychologists and sexual experts actually encourage couples to fantasize about other partners while in bed for the purpose of creating more passion in their sex life. **I couldn't disagree more.** That's like advising someone whose baby is crying to put on some loud music so they won't hear the poor infant's screams! There are reasons a couple stops experiencing passion in their sex life. (See Questions 2 and 47.) Adding fantasy to the relationship is a cover-up that distracts you from the real problem.

I also don't believe there's such a thing as "harmless fantasy." Sure, it may seem harmless to your husband, but it's obviously harming you. It shakes your sense of self-esteem; it hurts your sense of safety within the marriage; and it damages the trust between you. A committed relationship is a tremendous responsibility. *Every action, even every thought, affects the fabric of the marriage and the energy field that flows between the two partners.* Imagine your relationship like a bank. Each loving thought and deed is like a deposit that adds to your riches. Each nonloving thought or deed is a withdrawal. **When your husband invests his sexual and emotional energy in someone else's direction, even if the contact isn't physical, he is making a deposit elsewhere.** No wonder you feel somehow ripped off—you've been robbed of what should belong to you.

When one or both partners continue to invest their love energy in other directions, over time, they will find their relationship depleted of everything that was valuable. There have been too many withdrawals, and not enough deposits. This is why indulging in fantasy feeds into a vicious cycle. *The more people do it, the more they are going to need to do it.* At some point, fantasizing itself may not be enough, and they might need to actually have a physical affair.

Now, I'm not talking about the occasional thought about someone else that drifts into our mind in or out of bed. We're all human, and that can happen. I'm talking about consciously indulging in fantasy instead of making love to our mate. If you are someone who has come to rely on these mental dalliances in order to become aroused, ask yourself:

"Why has my passion for my partner diminished? Are we doing everything we can to keep our relationship emotionally healthy? Do we have some emotional tension that has built up between us, burying our passion?"

"Have I always been addicted to fantasy during sex? Is it my way of avoiding intimacy with my partner? Do I have some emotional programming that associates sex with particular images or circumstances so that this is the only way I can get turned on?" (See Questions 12 and 15.)

Let's give your husband the benefit of the doubt for a moment, and assume that he's been poorly programmed by society to indulge in all kinds of sexual habits that aren't healthy. *Perhaps he began his sex life as an adolescent fantasizing about women in magazines or girls at school, and never learned to transfer his erotic associations over onto his real live wife!* Share my answer to your question with him. Have a discussion about how you both feel. Hopefully, this information will enlighten him about how he is affecting you, and you can both commit to exploring new ways to build and maintain your sexual passion together. (If he still doesn't get it, I'd reevaluate this whole relationship, because I'll bet he isn't treating you respectfully in other areas either.)

SEE ALSO QUESTIONS 2, 12, 15, 37, AND 47

55 *What should a couple do when one wants to have sex much more often than the other?*

My husband is twenty-four and I'm twenty-one, and our problem is that we have very different sex drives. He likes to have sex once or twice a day, sometimes more, and I would be happy with once or twice a week. Is something wrong with me? Should I go along with it even though I don't feel like it?

━━❤❤❤━━ Did you say once or twice a day? Ouch . . . I'm exhausted just thinking about it. What you're describing is more than just a husband who can't keep his hands off you—it's sexual addiction. *Sexual addiction takes many forms, but one occurs in people who become addicted to sex as their primary means of releasing tension, expressing themselves, etc.* Usually, it occurs more in men than women, due to the differences in our physiology.

Here's how it works: Let's say your husband feels some strong emotions building up inside him. Maybe he's worried about a project at work. Maybe he just had an upsetting conversation with a friend, and he's hurt by what occurred. Maybe the feelings are positive, and he's experiencing tremendous love for you. **Many men aren't brought up to feel that it is okay to express vulnerable feelings such as fear, hurt, confusion, neediness, or even love. So either your partner won't feel safe expressing these emotions verbally, or he won't even know how to. And**

suddenly, he's in the mood for sex. He uses his sexual energy as a "safe" outlet for his repressed emotional energy.

Now I know this might not make much sense to you as a woman, since most (though not all) women function in the opposite way. We have a difficult time feeling sexual when we aren't feeling emotionally safe. *But it's important to understand that men use sex almost like a language to communicate their unspoken emotions.* At times, it's the only acceptable way some men allow themselves to feel anything at all. In your husband's case, he's quite young and is probably feeling the pressures of being newly married, trying to become successful, and just growing up in general. *It may be that reaching out for sex as often as he does is his way of reaching out to you for comfort and reassurance.*

As interesting as this may sound to you, you still have a problem . . . what to do about your horny hubby. First of all, *never, never "go along" with having sex when you don't want to.* You will end up feeling tremendous resentment, and eventually, you'll turn off to having sex completely. Besides, no matter how many times you have sex with him, I suspect that he's still not getting what he needs, which is why he has to keep doing it. *It's not the sexual satisfaction he's looking for—it's the love and acceptance, and the release of his emotional tension, which can only come from talking about his emotions.*

Here's what I suggest: Have your husband read

this section of the book, and ask for his opinion. Don't make him wrong by saying "See, I knew you were a sex addict!" Do say: "I want to make our relationship even better. What do you think of everything she says?" Talk about how you can make it more safe for him to release his emotional tension with words, and not just through sexual contact. Let him know you understand all the pressures he is under, and rather than judging him for his worries or concerns, you love him because he is so sensitive and responsible. *See if he will agree to check in with himself before he approaches you sexually, and notice whether he is feeling any anxiety. If he becomes aware of some tension, perhaps he can try talking about it before he decides he wants sex.* I believe if you are both willing to work on this, the intimacy in your relationship will increase, and when you do make love, it will be much more emotionally passionate.

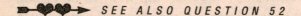 *SEE ALSO QUESTION 52*

56 Why can't my wife just have spontaneous sex sometimes?

I love making love to my wife, but feel kind of resentful about the "ordeal" I have to go through before we can have sex. First, my wife has to take a long bath, put on her favorite body lotion and who knows what else. Then, she has to set up the bedroom with candles all over the place, and the stereo has to be playing the perfect music. Finally, we have to go through this slow process of extended foreplay before we have intercourse. It's not that I'm against planning or romance, but it would be such a relief to just "do it" for a change. How can I get my wife to be more spontaneous?

━♥♥━ I hear you loud and clear, and by the way, you're not alone in your request for spontaneous sex. This is one of the most common complaints men have about women, and a big sexual turnoff. *Ladies, are you listening?* Let me explain why our insisting lovemaking always be a romantic ritual drives men crazy:

1. *When women prepare for sex as a major undertaking, it makes sex a project and puts performance pressure on men.* And men hate performance pressure—they already feel pressured to perform twenty-four hours a day. By the time you get out of the bathroom, or finish decorating the room, he feels as if

the spotlight has shifted onto him and he must live up to your anticipation.

2. *Men feel controlled when sex always has to be on your terms.* Look at it from his point of view. Your partner is turned on and wants to make love to you. You agree, and disappear into the bathroom for twenty minutes, making him wait. How does he feel? Controlled! And guess what? He's right! It's as if you're saying "I'll make love to you, but only if these conditions are met. . . ."

3. *When a woman never allows herself to have spontaneous sex, her partner concludes that she must not like sex very much since she can exert so much self-control.* He feels she must sanitize, idealize, and romanticize it in order to even enjoy it.

Now, in our defense, we often use the "romantic set-up" to get ourselves in the mood when our partner hasn't done the job for us. So guys, if you have neglected your wife's emotional needs all week, maybe she needs the bath and the candles to get herself ready because you didn't. And for those women brought up to feel having sex in itself is a little nasty, they may feel uncomfortable and out of control just giving in to their lust and "doing it." In fact, we often misinterpret our partner's just wanting to have sex with us, wrongly assuming that this means he doesn't feel as much for us as the other night when he did want to make more romantic love.

The truth is that men would be better lovers when they do make love to us if we gave them permission to not always have to make love each time we have sex. There is a certain kind of spontaneity, surrender, and passion that men experience when they allow themselves just to have sex with their mate, which is often lost in a more conscious, slow, step-by-step lovemaking process. Men actually crave this lustful surrender to us as intensely as we women crave the safety and tenderness of lovemaking. *(I'm not saying that, if your mate never makes love to you and always wants to just have quick sex, you should accept it. On the contrary, this is the kind of mistreatment you should never put up with.)*

For women, giving ourselves permission to have sex with our partner once in a while without doing it perfectly can be very liberating. So many of us try to "take the sex out of sex" in order to allow ourselves to have sex at all, and end up suppressing our natural sensuality. You may be surprised to find that, by the pure act of surrendering physically to your desire to unite with your partner, you become very aroused without the usual rituals. All of this advice, of course, is based on the assumption that the two of you have a healthy, loving relationship with no other obvious problems that could be causing conflict in your sex life.

As for you who asked the question, share this information with your wife. Ask her if she would be willing to try an experiment—**you promise to be the one to set up the romantic environment and initiate the extensive foreplay on one occasion if she's willing to just spontaneously grab you and say "I want you now" on the next occasion.** Sounds like a great deal to me . . . !

57 When is the right time to start being sexually intimate with a new partner?

I just met someone I really like, and we've been going out for a few weeks. We seem to be getting really close really fast, and there's a very strong physical attraction between us. When is the right time for us to make love? I don't want to rush things, but I don't want to lose this person either.

━━♥♥♥━▶ Stop . . . slow down . . . you hardly know this person. You may be a victim of *"lust blindness"*—in love with the feeling of passion, and not necessarily the person. You might simply have the hots for him or her. Then again, this may be the soul mate you've always been looking for. So . . . how can you tell which it is? How can you be sure you're not jumping into something that is all wrong? **YOU WAIT . . . YOU WATCH . . . AND YOU POSTPONE HAVING SEX UNTIL YOU CAN'T STAND IT ANY LONGER . . . AND THEN YOU POSTPONE IT AGAIN.**

One of the most common and most deadly mistakes many of us make in relationships is "premature intimacy." (See Question 33.) Several things happen when you have sex too soon in a relationship. *First, your judgment of your partner's character becomes blinded for a while, since you are sexually intoxicated.* It will be very difficult for you to be objective about the new relationship for months after you have sex. You're swept away by the lust, and perhaps only later do you see the warning signs of trouble you should have paid attention to in the beginning. *Second, you are mixing someone else's energy with yours without really checking him or her out first.* Sex is an intense sharing of mind, body, and spirit, whether you experience it that way or not. You are merging your energies with those of another person. Do you want to spiritually and psychically merge with just anyone? I didn't think so. *Third, becoming sexually intimate with someone has become a much more serious and possibly deadly undertaking in the past few decades than it used to be in the pre-AIDS era.* There is no 100-percent-risk-free sex, so you'd better be sure about your partner in every way possible.

Here are my guidelines for deciding when it's right to become sexual with someone:

- You should be *intellectually and emotionally intimate* before you are sexually intimate.
- You should spend at least *twice as much time* talking and learning about one another as you do necking or fooling around.
- You should *like* the person. I have a saying: DON'T SLEEP WITH SOMEONE YOU DON'T WANT TO BECOME LIKE.
- You should *respect* the person and his or her values.
- You should have gone through some difficult times together (one of you was sick, family crisis, job stress) and seen how your

partner operates under stress and how he or she treats you when you are under stress.

- You should have *discussed birth control, sexually transmitted diseases such as herpes and AIDS,* and know as much as possible about your partner's sexual history. If you haven't been tested for the AIDS virus, you should do so immediately, and insist that your partner do the same.

- You should have agreed on *what form of birth control and safe sex you are going to use.*

- If you are a woman, you should ask yourself: WOULD I WANT TO HAVE THIS MAN'S CHILDREN? and WOULD I WANT A SON JUST LIKE THIS MAN?

  These questions serve two purposes: first, they remind you that pregnancy is always a possibility, and will ensure that you are careful about birth control; and second, it will help you to be sure that you are ready to become sexually intimate with this man. Whether you actually want children or not, *if you don't like this man enough to want children that carry his genes, characteristics, and personality, then what are you doing sleeping with this guy?!!*

- If you are a man, you should ask yourself: WOULD I WANT THIS WOMAN TO BE THE MOTHER OF MY CHILDREN? . . . and

**... WOULD I WANT A DAUGHTER JUST
LIKE THIS WOMAN? Am I ready and willing to support a child if this woman became
pregnant?**

Now you may be thinking that I've taken all the
fun out of sex. My answer is: What's fun about getting your heart broken because it turns out the person you slept with is seeing someone else? What's
fun about lying in bed at night next to someone you
just made love with and feeling alone? What's fun
about having been sexually vulnerable with someone
only to find out that they lost interest after they got
you in bed? What's fun about an unwanted pregnancy? What's fun about finding out your partner
gave you herpes or HIV?

Making love can be one of the most beautiful
and healing experiences in the world when you experience it with the right person at the right time, but
I've seen it cause tremendous pain, humiliation, and
heartache for people who experience it with the
wrong person at the wrong time. *Having sex with
someone out of the fear of losing him or her is always a
mistake.* If this person is right for you, he or she will
understand and honor your wishes and values.

➡️💗💗➡️ SEE ALSO QUESTIONS 26
AND 33

58 *Is it possible for a couple to rediscover their sexual desire for one another after it has disappeared?*

My husband and I need help! After eighteen years, and four children, the passion between us has disappeared. We rarely have sex, and our relationship is sort of comfortable, but boring. Is this just the way marriage is supposed to be, or is there a way we can somehow rekindle our desire for each other?

➤━❤❤━➤ YES, it's possible to rekindle the passion. NO, this isn't just the way marriage is supposed to be. Before going any further, go back and read the answers to Question 2, Question 7, and Question 47. Then ask your husband to read them with you. The information should give you a pretty good idea of why two people who love each other and want a relationship to work can still end up feeling that the sexual attraction has disappeared.

One of the most frightening feelings in the world is waking up next to your partner in the morning and, as you watch him sleep, realizing that you aren't attracted to him anymore. **Remember: Often the chemistry isn't gone—it's just buried underneath piles of unexpressed feelings and bad habits. With hard work and emotional retraining, it's possible not only to rediscover the passion, but to experience more love and intimacy than you did before.**

Sex is really just a mirror for us—a mirror that reflects the state of our mind, our heart, and our soul.

Ultimately, sexual chemistry is really just the reso-
nance of your being and your partner's on the physical, mental, emotional, and spiritual levels. The
more you resonate similarly on these levels, the more
sexual attraction you will feel. There are times, therefore, when the chemistry disappears because you
and your partner have grown in separate directions
and become highly incompatible. If you and your
partner begin to resonate on very different vibra-
tional levels, you will not feel attracted to one another anymore.

**This is an important point to understand—it's
not that you stop feeling attracted to your partner
and therefore the relationship stops working. It's
that you stopped feeling attracted to your partner
because the relationship stopped working. When
you and your partner stop resonating physically,
emotionally, intellectually, or spiritually, you will
stop resonating sexually.**

If you and your mate are committed to doing
everything it takes to make your relationship work,
and still feel a lot of compatibility in other nonsexual
areas of your marriage, don't give up. It's never too
late for a new beginning.

➤❤❤❤➤ *SEE ALSO QUESTIONS 2, 7,
37, AND 47*

How can a couple with children maintain a spontaneous, exciting sex life?

I think my partner and I have a great marriage, but with two small children, spontaneous sex seems to be a thing of the past. Do you have any ideas that can help us have the kind of exciting sex life we used to before the kids were born?

▰❤❤▰ If I answered, *"Yes, your sex life can be just as spontaneous and wild as it was when you lived alone in your house with no children crying, fighting, playing, getting sick, asking questions, pulling on you for attention, tiring you out during the day, and wandering into your room at night,"* you'd think I was full of it . . . and you'd be right! As any parent knows, children change everything in your life, including your sexual relationship. And although it certainly isn't easy, it is important that you maintain a healthy and passionate sex life.

The key is *"planning for spontaneity."* You already know that with children in the house, you've lost the freedom you used to have to seize the moment and have passionate sex whenever you wanted to. If you wait for those moments to come, you may have to wait forever . . . well, at least for many years. *Instead, you can plan time during which spontaneous passion can occur.*

For instance, arrange to leave your children with a friend or relative for a few hours on a weekend afternoon. *You and your partner know ahead of time that*

*this is your afternoon to be alone together. That doesn't
necessarily mean you will have sex—it means you want to
share some intimate moments, focusing only on each other,
and not the children.* You might end up taking a walk,
cuddling on the couch in front of an old movie, giving each other a massage, or just holding each other
and enjoying the quiet. **In that special time, many
things will spontaneously happen, and one of them
might be sex.**

I know some couples who hire a baby-sitter to
come over and watch the kids, or take them out to a
park, so that the parents can enjoy some private time
in their own home without worrying about what the
kids are doing. Others trade off with friends who also
have children. You will have to be creative, but the
idea is to not only plan but schedule time into your
week or month, in the same way you'd schedule an
appointment with the dentist . . . only this appointment is with your lover (and will probably be much
more pleasurable!).

Don't forget that what makes this work is that
*you are **not** planning to have sex; you are planning to
spend private time together.* Couples often make the
mistake of planning a few hours alone and deciding
ahead of time that they will have sex. This not only
puts a lot of pressure on you to instantly be in the
mood, but doesn't give you the opportunity to discover your desire for one another in the moment.
When you plan to share intimate time, with no pre-

conceived notions of what will happen, you create the space for your natural attraction to rise up (no pun intended) and for the passion to grow out of your love, just as it would when you spent time together pre-kids.

One word of caution, especially to overprotective mothers: this plan requires some letting go on your part, especially of your concern that your children cannot possibly be all right unless you are there with them twenty-four hours a day. Choose your caregivers carefully, and then relax—the kids will be fine. More importantly, you will learn that they can survive without you (sad but true, Moms!) and in the process, you will have a chance to fall in love with your husband all over again.

60 How can I overcome some childhood sexual trauma and have a normal sex life?

I was sexually molested as a young child, and I'm having a hard time opening up physically with my husband of six months. I love him dearly, but I often freeze up in bed. He's being very patient, but I know how frustrated he is. Could my childhood trauma be affecting me? How can I increase my sex drive?

▶━♥♥━▶ Of course your childhood trauma is affecting you. For you, as with most victims of childhood sexual abuse, the experience of sex is associated with powerlessness, betrayal, fear, loss of control, anger, confusion, shame, and remorse. Remember, most of our emotional programming occurs when we are quite young (see Question 12), and in your case, your unconscious mind was bombarded with negative images relating to sexual activity. *So naturally, when you get into bed with your husband, your psyche gets flooded with emotional flashbacks. All those unexpressed emotions and reactions from the past overwhelm you, and you "freeze up," a perfect choice of words, since a part of you is frozen in time.*

I know how awful you feel loving your husband and being unable to open up to him. Please understand that your lack of sexual drive has absolutely nothing to do with how hard you try to feel it, or how much you care about your husband, or how much he tries to make you feel safe. **Emotionally, you're a**

prisoner of the past. You put up walls to protect yourself from the pain of what you experienced, walls that keep you feeling numb. You had no choice. Now, it's time to heal the pain you've kept locked inside those walls, and melt the ice around your heart.

Tell your husband you're ready to face the demons you've run from all these years, that his love has made you feel strong enough and safe enough to go to battle and conquer the ghosts from the past. Then, find a qualified therapist who specializes in recovery from childhood sexual abuse. One step at a time, you will reclaim the pieces of the power you lost, and with each piece you will discover new strength and new feeling. Before you know it, you will be free to share your love for your husband completely, and to receive his love completely.

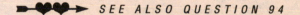 *SEE ALSO QUESTION 94*

How can I tell my partner I don't like the way he makes love to me?

I have a really sensitive problem. I love my husband, but can't stand the way he makes love. I almost never enjoy sex and rarely have an orgasm. I've tried to give him suggestions about what he can do to please me, but he just doesn't get it. How can I get through to him without being blunt and making him feel he's doing it wrong?

➤❤❤❤➤ *You can't. You have to be blunt—otherwise he isn't going to get it, is he?* He hasn't so far. Hinting isn't working. You're going to have to be a lot more specific and give him lots of details, very intimate and clinical details. You may even have to show him. (You won't be the first woman who's done it . . . !)

Now, can you do this without making him feel he's been doing it wrong? Well, let's put it this way . . . there are ways to say what you have to say without blaming him: *"Look honey, I know I'm a woman and you're a man, so believe me, I don't expect you to understand my anatomy and physiology. In fact, I should have explained some of this to you sooner. . . ."* The question is, will he buy this? I doubt it. **After all, the fact is, he *has* been doing it all wrong, hasn't he?** You can't very well pretend he's been a terrific lover while you're drawing him a picture of your vagina and pointing out the clitoris.

I guess what I'm saying is, *stop worrying about protecting his feelings, and say what you have to say as best as you can.* After all, you've been worrying about hurting him for all this time, and what good has it done you, or him for that matter? Do you think he would have wanted you to pretend he was pleasing you rather than bruising his ego? No, so get the unpleasant conversation over with already!

P.S. Don't bring this up while you're in bed having sex. Bad idea . . . Let him know you want to have a serious talk, set a time, and discuss it then. (You may, however, need a demonstration lesson or two in bed, once he's gotten over the shock of your announcement. Hey, it could even be fun!)

62 Why is it that men don't know how to touch women the right way and in the right places?

Is something wrong with men, or is it just me? I've never been married, but I've had several serious relationships, and every man I've been with hasn't had a clue about how to please me sexually. They don't seem to know their way around my private parts at all, and end up touching me the wrong way in the wrong places. Do I have to draw these guys a map?

➤━❤❤❤━➤ This is a different version of Question 61, but I hear it just as much. And the answer is: YES, YOU MIGHT HAVE TO DRAW THESE GUYS A MAP! Do you know why that is? *Because they don't have one, so they don't know what it feels like, or how it works, and unless some other bold woman before you has educated them they have no way of figuring it out for themselves.*

Ladies, I know we've all had that awfully frustrating, teeth-gnashing, experience of lying there while our beloved diligently and passionately touches our vagina in the *wrong* place for a lonnnnng, lonnnnng, ever so long time. We squirm hopefully to the left, to the right, forwards, backwards, hoping that simply by the process of elimination, his untrained fingers will land on our anxiously waiting clitoris. But nooo, somehow, in spite of all of our yogic contortions, he stubbornly misses just where he should be touching, and annoyingly grinds into some unmanned spot on our female geography (now totally numb), all the time wondering why we aren't writhing yet in ecstasy.

Well, here's the deal. Think about a penis for a moment. It's big. It sticks out. It has a huge surface area. And you can touch just about anywhere on it and it will feel fantastic to the owner. Now your man knows that. In fact, he's probably touched himself many times, usually without focusing on any particular spot. Pleasuring himself doesn't require much skill. He just grabs the whole thing and he's a happy camper. *In other words, unless someone informs him otherwise, he sees your vagina as a differently shaped penis; thus, his lack of manual exactitude.*

It is your job to inform your man that God did not create all things equal, and that, unlike the generous size of your sweetheart's very sensitive penis, your clitoris is perhaps only one-quarter of an inch large, and, in fact, may be hidden from view entirely. Not only that, it is a very temperamental little piece of flesh, and cannot be handled as casually as one would fondle a penis. In fact, there are a whole series of other places that probably need to be touched properly before your clitoris even wants to be touched.

Believe me, with proper education (and, for the mechanically challenged male, an actual demonstration), you'll soon find that the time you invested in this remedial tour of your private parts was well spent. Enjoy.

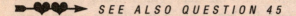 *SEE ALSO QUESTION 45*

Why do men experience premature ejaculation?

I've been dating a really wonderful man for about six months, and we've just started having sex. Unfortunately, he has a problem with premature ejaculation. At first, I thought it was just the newness of the relationship, or the fact that he was recovering from an ugly divorce. But it still happens just about every time. We've talked about it briefly, and he feels just as badly as I do. What can cause this? Is there anything I can do to help?

➤❤❤❤➤ Most men experience difficulty with premature or "early" ejaculation at some point in their lives. Early ejaculation occurs because there is a buildup of sexual tension in the body that demands release earlier than the male (and usually the female) would like it to be released. If the problem is chronic, it can be a source of tremendous frustration to both partners. Here are some common causes of early ejaculation:

- *Improper lovemaking techniques:* **Early ejaculation occurs when a man is too tense physically, mentally, or emotionally.** This can be due to poor lovemaking habits such as trying to get turned on too much too quickly, tensing the buttocks in order to intensify the pleasure, or rushing to get to orgasm. There are many excellent books that discuss techniques for

handling the sexual tension during lovemaking so it doesn't release too soon. I would also
suggest you read my first book *How to Make
Love All the Time* and learn about "Gourmet
Sex" versus "Greedy Sex." Often men who
practice "greedy sex," trying to experience as
much pleasure as quickly as possible, end up
overloading the body and become victims of
early ejaculation.

- *Withholding emotions from a partner:* Holding
  back causes tension. Ever try to hold back a
  laugh, or hold back tears? It hurts to hold
  back. The same goes for holding back feelings. *Holding back feelings creates an emotional
  tension that then causes tension in the body. If
  your partner is holding back feelings of anger,
  guilt, or fear when he is making love to you, or has
  a secret he hasn't told you, he will have more of a
  tendency to ejaculate quickly.* The holding back
  creates tension which makes lasting longer
  very difficult. Men who have a hard time
  communicating or sharing their emotions often have problems with premature ejaculation. (These emotions may even be positive,
  such as love or need, so don't conclude that
  your partner necessarily is suppressing unpleasant emotions.)

- *Fear of or dislike for sex:* If your partner was
  ever sexually molested, or taught that sex was

dirty, he may "rush" through lovemaking in order to get it over with. It's as if his penis says *"Let's come and get out of here in a hurry."*

- *History of having sex with women he didn't love:* If your partner has a history of sleeping with women he didn't care for, or visiting prostitutes, he may find it difficult to take his time making love to you. His penis is in the habit of making "quick departures."

- *Fear of intimacy:* Premature ejaculation can be the way your partner's body responds to the fear of getting too close during sex. Coming quickly ensures that he won't spend too much time loving you.

Although this list may help you understand some of the causes of premature ejaculation, reading it certainly isn't going to change your partner's sexual performance. I know how sensitive this topic is for both of you, but you need to discuss it honestly and thoroughly. Encourage your mate to seek some professional help from a qualified therapist who will guide him in exploring the sexual and emotional issues mentioned above. If he's unwilling to confront this problem, you should reconsider remaining involved in what at this point is still a new relationship.

64 *Is it okay for my husband to look at porno magazines?*

My husband and I have an ongoing battle about his habit of constantly reading porno magazines. I feel like it's wrong, and that he shouldn't need them now that we're married. He says all men do it, that it's "no big deal," and I'm overreacting. It's starting to ruin our sex life, because I feel so angry and turned off to him. Should I just try to accept it, or should I take a stand?

➠💗💗➠ I don't know about you, but I can't imagine lying in bed next to my husband while he gazed lustfully at pictures of naked women, and telling myself, "You should just accept this. It's no big deal." In fact, when most women are honest with themselves, they admit that when their husband reads porno magazines, or goes to strip clubs or calls 900 sex numbers, they feel cheated on, and I wholeheartedly agree. *Regularly indulging in sexual fantasy about other people, whether in one's mind, through reading magazines or watching films, is a form of infidelity. You have made a commitment to be sexually monogamous with your partner, and you break it by deliberately focusing your sexual attention on someone else.*

Intimacy is the shared experience of closeness and connection between two people. Sexual pornography destroys intimacy because, by definition, it introduces a third element into your relationship—

the thought or picture or video of another person or sexual situation. Although some couples claim they both enjoy sharing pornography together, I strongly doubt that it creates more intimacy in the long run. **What it does do is create more eroticism, which many couples mistake for intimacy.**

The reason your husband feels justified in claiming that his porno mag habit is harmless is that, in my opinion, our society has an enormous, sexist double standard when it comes to this issue: it overlooks, minimizes, and even supports milder forms of pornography such as the *Sports Illustrated* swimsuit issue or commercials that sell beer by using bikini-clad women, while claiming at the same time to disapprove of so-called hard-core pornography. Men like your husband are victims/participants in this double standard, and unfortunately, it is we as their wives and girlfriends who suffer because of it, as you well know.

It's not that your husband or men who read porno magazines are "bad." But their behavior will be disruptive to the intimacy and safety of the relationship.

- *You will feel "cheated on" by your partner because he needs something other than you in order to become aroused.*
- *You will feel insecure about your body, your sexuality, and your ability to satisfy your partner.*

- *You will feel emotionally distant and separate from your partner during sex, worrying that he is not completely "there" with you.*
- *You will feel angry and resentful toward your partner for not respecting your feelings.*
- *You will eventually feel turned off to sex, since for you, it is associated with humiliation, control, and a feeling of inadequacy.*

In spite of what your husband says, I don't consider his habit "harmless" if it's creating these reactions in you. He may not mean it to be harmful. I'm sure he loves you very much, and truly doesn't want to hurt you. But the reality is, he is hurting you. Don't let yourself get talked out of your feelings. Trust your instincts. *It's not a question of what is normal and what is not. It's a question of what is healthy or unhealthy for your relationship, and you already know that in this case, your relationship is suffering.*

See if your husband will read this section of the book, as well as Question 54. **Remember—don't make him wrong for what he is doing. Simply share how his behavior makes you feel.** Ask him how he would feel if you sat around admiring the financial assets, luxury homes, and lavish lifestyles of wealthy men in a magazine about really successful people. I don't think he'd enjoy coming home from a hard day at the office where he is working hard to try and make a good living, only to find you drooling over some man who had everything he didn't. I don't think he'd appreciate comments like *"Boy, this guy is soooo impressive. Look at how successful he is. He must really be smart. I just love a man who is good with money."* (Kind of the equivalent of "look at those breasts.")

If nothing gets through to him, then it's time for some professional help. Your marriage is already going through the Four R's. (See Question 47.) It's time for some emotional first-aid.

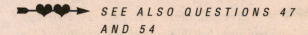 *SEE ALSO QUESTIONS 47 AND 54*

65 How can I get my partner to slow down during sex?

My boyfriend and I have been together for two years, and our relationship is very satisfying except in the sexual area. We have a lot of passion, but he goes so fast during love-making that the whole thing only lasts about five minutes from the first kiss to the finish! I want him to slow down, but don't know how to tell him without making him feel criticized. How can I get him to take more time? Or is this length of time normal?

▶♥♥▶ Five minutes? Did you say five minutes? Is he trying to break a record or something? You asked me if this is normal, which tells me that you don't have very much sexual experience, or you would know that this guy is going *way too fast*. Five minutes into lovemaking, he should still be kissing you and getting cozy, not getting up to take a shower.

I'm assuming that your boyfriend is young, and that his speedy approach to sex comes from his boyish enthusiasm and lack of understanding of what women really need. So let's give him the benefit of the doubt. (If he's forty years old, on the other hand, you have a bigger problem!) And by the way, you said "five minutes from the first kiss to the finish." I'll bet anything you mean *his* finish, and not yours . . . most women need a bit more time than that . . . !

So, to your boyfriend, and men everywhere, here's an important piece of sexual advice based on years of extensive research: **SLOW DOWN!!! Stop approaching having sex with your lover as if you're trying to get it over with. This isn't a race. You don't get extra points for finishing quickly. In fact, the opposite is true—the longer you take, the better it will be for her, and for you too!**

Here's another word to memorize: *FOREPLAY! You know what it means. Don't get lazy or selfish and skip it.* You wouldn't put your car into fourth gear directly from first, would you? No, the car would stall. So why would you take your lover for a "ride" without warming her up first by running through all her gears? (See Question 52.)

Now, about pacing yourself: Imagine you're eating a delicious and very expensive seven-course meal prepared by a master chef. Would you gobble it down as fast as you could? No, hopefully, you would do what all food gourmets do—you would eat slowly, savoring each bite, allowing time for the food to digest before you went on to the next course.

This is how you should make love, like a gourmet. Instead of trying to stuff as much pleasure and energy into your genitals as quickly as possible so that your body finally has to release it within a few minutes in the form of a quick orgasm, try having **gourmet sex.** *Make love slowly, taking time to get used to all that intense sexual energy. Let your body "digest" or integrate the energy.*

When you feel the sexual energy building up in your body, don't race ahead to push yourself

over the edge into orgasm. Instead: PAUSE . . .
BREATHE . . . Allow your body to become accus-
tomed to the intensity of the physical sensation before you begin moving again. It may seem like you're
doing nothing. But if you let your awareness sink
deeper into the silence between your movements,
and focus on the love energy flowing between you
and your partner, rather than on your own arousal,
you will find yourself relaxing.

When you're ready, you can begin moving together again. *You'll find that you're now able to handle
even more pleasure and stimulation without feeling like
you need to release it,* and that the waves just keep getting bigger and bigger. **The better you get at staying
in the moment, and the longer you allow the sexual
energy to circulate in your body before releasing it,
the greater your physical and emotional ecstasy
will become. Sounds delicious, doesn't it? It is. . . .**

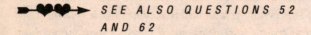 *SEE ALSO QUESTIONS 52
AND 62*

66

How can I get my partner to do more than just lie there during sex?

My problem is that my girlfriend just lies there during sex like a log. She hardly moves, she doesn't make a sound, and I can't tell if she is bored, turned off, or just numb. When I ask her how she's feeling, she answers "Fine." How can I get her to respond to me so I don't feel like I might as well be having sex by myself?

━━♥♥━━ I call the kind of partner you're describing *"The Sexual Corpse"—you feel like you're making love to a dead person, don't you?* You end up feeling inadequate for not satisfying her, selfish since she doesn't seem to be enjoying herself, controlled by her lack of response, and, eventually, turned off emotionally and sexually.

First, make sure your girlfriend doesn't have a serious psychological problem, such as a history of sexual abuse, that's making it difficult for her to enjoy sex. (See Question 60.) Ask her to read the answer, and tell you if it relates to her situation. She may need professional help in order to feel comfortable with her sexuality.

Let's assume, however, that your girlfriend doesn't have any problems with sexual dysfunction. Why would she be lying there "like a log"? **Well, she either doesn't like sex, she doesn't want to admit she likes sex, or she doesn't like sex with you!** (See Question 53.) How can you tell which of these is going on? Ask her. In fact, let her know your relationship is undergoing a crisis, and you need to understand her experience before you can go forward. Hopefully, she will be honest with herself and you and will share her secrets. *If she refuses to talk about it and continues to withhold, you should think about ending this relationship, because it is only going to bring you increasing pain.*

Don't forget to work on your own issues (see Question 15), and ask yourself why you attracted a partner who cannot show you love. You deserve to know that your woman loves to make love with you!

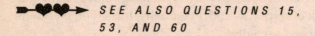 *SEE ALSO QUESTIONS 15,*
53, AND 60

67

How can I learn to have an orgasm when my partner and I make love? What does it mean if I can't?

Is there something wrong with me if I've never had an orgasm during sex? My boyfriend has tried everything, but in spite of how much I love him, I can't have an orgasm when we make love. Even though he acts patient, I know he is frustrated. I'm so embarrassed that now I'm avoiding sex entirely. I've only had two sexual relationships in my life, but it's happened both times. What can I do?

━━●♥♥► Don't be embarrassed—statistics tell us that over half of all women experience difficulty achieving orgasm, and a smaller percentage of women have never experienced orgasm, so you are certainly not alone. Let's look at all aspects of your situation and see if we can come up with some suggestions.

First of all, there are three categories you may fall into, and you need to decide which one is accurate:

1. *You have never had an orgasm at all.*

There are two very personal questions you need to answer: *Have you ever masturbated? Have you ever brought yourself to orgasm?* If you haven't masturbated, then you don't know whether or not your body is capable of experiencing orgasm, what orgasm actually feels like, or how to "cooperate" with your boyfriend by using your own muscles during sex to create more pleasure for yourself. You also won't know what works for your body, so you won't be able to communicate this to your boyfriend. *If this is the case, you need to experiment on your own before you worry about improving your sex life with your mate.* You will probably feel relieved to discover that you can experience orgasm, and that the problem lies in the next category.

If you have tried self-stimulation, but haven't been able to achieve orgasm on your own, then you'll need to focus on healing yourself, rather than on fixing your boyfriend's sexual style. There are several reasons why women may be nonorgasmic on their own:

- *Anger:* I would say that suppressed anger and rage is one of the main causes for a woman's inability to achieve orgasm. Anger doesn't allow us to feel pleasure. Women who have been molested or raped, women who have been abandoned or unloved or cheated on, may have so much anger locked inside of them that it prevents them from feeling joy and passion.

- *Guilt or shame:* If you were brought up in a strict religious background, you may have been taught that self-stimulation is a sin, and that the purpose of sex is for procreation, and not pleasure. This programming may be so much a part of you that your body "refuses" to respond, even when you think you want it to. You may also feel shame due to childhood sexual abuse about any pleasure you experienced, and have unconsciously decided that you are not "allowed" to experience pleasure in that part of your body anymore.

- *Fear of being controlled and going out of control:* Being in control is the opposite of orgasm, which is a total letting go. If a woman has a problem with control, is feeling controlled by her partner or has felt victimized by men in the past, she may have a difficult time "losing control" enough to have an orgasm.

- *Dietary causes:* Sexual excitement is caused by blood flow, and if your diet is too high in fat, you may have a sluggish circulatory system, making it difficult for you to experience sexual arousal and orgasm.

If any of this rings true for you, please seek help from a qualified sex therapist who will support you in safely exploring the psychological issues underlying your sexual problem.

2. *You have had orgasms by yourself, but never with a partner.*

If you know your body is capable of experiencing orgasm, but that you don't when you are with a man, one of two things is happening. *Either you've chosen partners who don't know what they are doing sexually, and therefore, can't bring you to orgasm, or, you have psychological issues such as the ones listed above that don't allow you to let go sexually in the presence of a man.* Some women have no problem experiencing orgasm through self-stimulation. They are in control and feel safe. However, often these same women cannot climax with a partner, in spite of how skilled he is as a lover.

I suspect that this is your situation, since you said you couldn't climax with your previous partner either. I encourage you to seek professional help to heal the issues underlying the sexual problem. You deserve to know the complete joy and surrender making love can give you, so it's time to find out what's preventing that from happening.

3. *You have had orgasms with other partners, but not with this partner.*

I know this isn't your situation, but it happens to many women. You know you are orgasmic, but you find yourself involved with a man who just can't get you off! Ask yourself: *Does he need some education about how to satisfy me?* (See Question 52, Question 61, and Question 62.) *Do I really want to be with this guy?* Maybe your body is being more honest with you than your intellect, and is telling you something you need to hear.

Finally, be patient with yourself. Discovering and honoring our sexuality is a lifelong adventure for women. And the older we get, the better it gets!

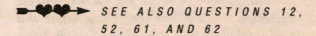 *SEE ALSO QUESTIONS 12, 52, 61, AND 62*

68 *How can I get my wife to give me more oral sex?*

My wife enjoys receiving oral sex, but almost never offers to reciprocate. I've told her I really would like to have her make love to me in this way, but she says she's "not into it." What does that mean? How can I get her to try it more often?

➤❤❤❤➤ You and millions of other men in the world would like the answer to this question. Let me try to explain what's going on here. First of all, when your wife says she's "not into it," she could mean a variety of things, none of which she's anxious to actually verbalize, which is why she's being vague. But believe me, although she may sound vague, what she's feeling inside isn't vague. I know, because when I wrote my book *Secrets About Men Every Woman Should Know*, I interviewed hundreds of women about their feelings regarding oral sex, and boy, did they talk!

Here's some of what women who don't enjoy it feel about oral sex that they don't tell the men in their lives.

1. They think it is disgusting.

One of the biggest mistakes women make when imagining giving oral sex to a man is thinking, "*Ugh! Giving him oral sex means I have to stick this guy's dick in my mouth, and that's the same place he pees from! Gross!"* Sorry—that's what goes on in a woman's mind.

2. They think it's dirty.

A continuation of the above theme: *"Ugh! I don't want to put that thing in my mouth. It's probably all dirty, sweaty, and smelly."*

3. They are afraid they will gag.

"What if he sticks it in so far that I gag and throw up all over him?"

4. They are afraid you will ejaculate in their mouth.

"What if he comes in my mouth? I'll choke on it, or throw up! Yuk—I'll bet it tastes horrible. Oh no, I can't swallow that. But I can't spit it all over him either. Forget it—I don't want to think about it anymore."

5. They are afraid you will think they are a bad type of girl.

"Only whores do that. That's the kind of thing guys pay for, isn't it? Somehow it's sleazy."

I'm not saying these concerns all make sense, or are fair, or logical, or that there aren't solutions for each one of them. All I'm telling you, guys, is that this is what a woman means when she says "I'm not into it."

However, we know that men *are* into it, and ladies, you need to understand why they love receiving oral sex so much. A man's penis is not only the most sensitive part of his body, but the most vulnerable. It represents his maleness, his sense of power, his identity. *Men don't love oral sex just because it feels so good—they love it because it makes them feel so accepted, so received.* It is the only sexual act during which he can be totally passive, and you become the aggressor. You give, and he receives, experiencing a more feminine, receptive mode.

When I teach women about how to give oral sex to their partners (See *Secrets About Men Every Woman Should Know,* Chapter Five), I remind them that the key is to imagine their partner is only about six inches tall, the size of the average penis. Instead of thinking "I'm loving his dick!" imagine loving a miniature version of your mate, as if all he was could be contained within the size and shape of a penis. Suddenly, you're not giving him a blow job—you're loving and adoring an expression of your sweetheart.

Talk with your wife about all of this information. Try not to be offended at anything she says, and make suggestions that will help remedy her concerns. For instance, if she's concerned about hygiene, suggest she try a little oral sex right after you've taken a shower. Share your experience of loving her orally, and how much special intimacy it creates for you. *Perhaps she'd be willing to experiment with loving you orally a minute at a time, practicing the technique I suggested.* I have a feeling that the more open and frank you are with her, the more open she'll be to re-examining her feelings about oral sex.

➤❤❤❤➤ *SEE ALSO QUESTIONS 53 AND 56*

69 What can I do to really please my husband in bed?

►❤❤► Simple: Ask *him* (not me!): "Honey, what can I do to *really* please you in bed?" I have a feeling he will be glad you asked and won't hesitate a bit in answering!

Cheating
and
Infidelity

I just found out that my husband of fifteen years has been cheating on me. I've suspected this for a while, but wasn't sure until a friend confessed that she knew about it. I confronted him with the information, but he still totally denies it. Should I try to keep my family together and hope he will get over this?

━❤❤❤➤ What do you hope that your husband will "get over"—his total disrespect for your feelings, his flagrant dishonesty, his moral weakness, his selfishness, his denial, or his lack of morality? Wake up and face the facts! Not only is he having an affair and breaking your marriage vows, but when confronted, he doesn't even have the courage and decency to tell you the truth! He is treating you like dirt. You know it, and he knows it.

Here's the real question you should be asking yourself: *"Why do I want to stay with a man who is behaving in this disgusting manner toward me? Why do I want to remain married to someone who obviously doesn't care enough about me to be honest?"* Remember—affairs are symptoms of a relationship *already* in trouble. Even before the infidelity, I have no doubt that there have been some significant problems in your marriage, whether you acknowledge them or not. So ask yourself, is this marriage as it truly is, not as you wish it would be, worth saving?

Or has it been over for a while, and you just haven't admitted it to yourself?

Most woman have such deeply rooted issues about abandonment that we often instinctively try to cling on to the man in our life, regardless of how he treats us or how unhealthy our relationship might be. **Our fear of loss overrides our fear of being hurt or humiliated.** Thus, we stay with men we should leave, put up with behavior we shouldn't tolerate, and feel we will be successful if we "keep the marriage together," even if that marriage is totally dysfunctional.

I think, in part, this is what's happening to you. You speak about "keeping your family together." So I ask you, *what does that really mean?* That you all get to live in the same house, even though your heart is broken? That none of your friends or family will think there is a problem because there won't be an "official separation"? That your kids will mistakenly believe everything is fine as long as Daddy doesn't move out, even though Daddy's out screwing someone else?? That's not my idea of "together." What you are describing is called *"denial."*

If you want to be a good mother to your children and a loving caretaker to your own inner self, you will inform your husband that he has to move out immediately—no discussion, no excuses, no negotiation. By lying and cheating, he has lost his right to live with you as his wife and live in the house as part of the family. Perhaps being kicked out will wake him up out of his stupor and help him to see the light. If this occurs, he confesses the truth, and begs for another chance, you can consider the possibility that you may be able to resurrect your relationship only under the following conditions:

WHAT TO DO WHEN YOU'VE BEEN CHEATED ON:

1. **You and your partner physically separate immediately. If you wish to stay in your home, he should be the one who must leave.**

2. **If he wants another chance, he must immediately break off all contact with his mistress—no phone calls, no letters, nothing.**

3. **He must immediately enter intensive therapy in order to determine why he had the affair, to understand what problems within himself and the marriage caused him to cheat.**

4. **You must also immediately enter intensive therapy in order to determine why you ignored the warning signs of his infidelity for so long, to deal with your feelings of anger and betrayal, and to take an honest look at the relationship.**

5. If, after some time, you both feel you are seeing your relationship through new eyes and think there might be a chance for reconciliation, you will need to enter intensive therapy together.

6. If after undergoing intensive therapy together, you both feel you have learned enough to understand how your relationship fell apart and feel willing to try again, you will need to start from the beginning. *YOU CANNOT GO BACK TO THE OLD RELATIONSHIP. IT IS DEAD. IT FAILED. YOU MUST START FROM SCRATCH, BUILDING A NEW RELATIONSHIP JUST AS ANY COUPLE DOES.* This means you continue living apart and begin to date, getting to know one another again. You have new ground rules, new goals for yourselves individually and for the relationship, and new skills with which to create healthy communication and intimacy. You take it slowly, and see how it goes.

I cannot emphasize strongly enough how important it is to follow these guidelines if you wish to salvage a relationship that has ended in infidelity. And I know how difficult it may sound, and how much courage you will need to stick to your resolve when

your husband is crying and pleading with you to forgive him, *but don't give in.* The only chance you have
of experiencing a true and complete healing on this
issue is to see the situation as it truly is, and to start
treating yourself with the love and respect you
would hope one day to receive from the man you
love.

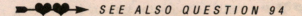 **SEE ALSO QUESTION 94**

71 Should you give a cheating partner another chance?

My boyfriend of nine months just confessed that he had a brief affair with an old flame a few months ago. He promised me he would never do it again and begged me to take him back. We've been having a lot of problems lately, but I really love him. Would I be stupid to give him another chance?

━━♥♥━➤ Well, let's give the guy credit for being honest with you. At least he feels remorse, knows what he did was wrong, and doesn't want to lose you. You're several steps ahead of the woman in Question 70, although you're going to have to follow the same path to recovery. You said it yourself—you've been having problems lately, so you know that the affair is just a reflection of underlying issues you can no longer ignore.

No, you wouldn't be stupid to give your boyfriend another chance. An affair doesn't have to signify the end of a relationship. *In fact in some cases, if both partners are willing to work hard, an affair can bring problems that were lurking in the depths of the relationship up to the surface for the purpose of healing.* Since your relationship is relatively new, it's likely that you are both still settling into your commitment to one another, or at least he is! And it sounds like he may be having some difficulty letting go completely of his former lover (see Question 29). So if he is sincere, and you feel he's worth it, and you can let go of what happened (not easy!), it's possible that you could both use this crisis to stop, evaluate the relationship, and go forward differently.

You still to need to follow the guidelines in Question 70. *His saying "I'm sorry" isn't enough. Just because he's not cheating on you anymore doesn't mean the problem has disappeared—it hasn't. It's still there, but it's in remission.* Don't delude yourself into believing the coast is clear now that he's apparently being faithful again. Stand your ground, and insist on going through a modified version of my Cheating Recovery Program outlined earlier. If this guy really loves you and truly doesn't want to lose you, he'll thank his lucky stars that you're willing to give him another chance, and will work his butt off to get to the bottom of the situation.

►♥♥► *SEE ALSO QUESTIONS 29, 37, AND 70*

After twenty years of marriage and four children, my husband told me that he had a one night stand last month while on a business trip. I don't know if he would have confessed on his own, but he was acting so guilty, that I knew something was wrong, and when I confronted him, he admitted it. He insists that he didn't plan it, that "it just happened," and that "it didn't mean anything." What does a man mean when he says that? Am I being old-fashioned or stubborn to feel outraged?

First of all, let me scream . . . AAA-AAARRRRRRGGGGGGHHH! Whew, I needed that. Sorry, but whenever I hear someone claim that his sexual infidelity "just happened," I react like this. *What does your husband mean by "it just happened"?* Does he expect you to believe that one night, during a business convention, he "just happened" to be walking down the hallway of his hotel when a door to someone's room "just happened" to open, and a strong gust of wind "just happened" to blow your husband into the room where a beautiful woman "just happened" to be lying on the bed naked with her legs spread, and your husband bumped into a chair and "just happened" to get knocked onto the bed, and his fly "just happened" to be down, and, oh yes, he was thinking about you at the time so he "just happened" to have a huge erection which, because of everything else that "just happened," plunged instantly into the naked woman's vagina . . . is this what he means?

Infidelity doesn't just happen. There were many moments when your husband made the decision to do things he shouldn't have done. Mistake Number One: He decided to spend time with a woman he found sexually attractive. Mistake Number Two: He decided to indulge in flirtatious behavior and sexual innuendo with this woman. Mistake Number Three: He decided to go up to a hotel room with this woman. Mistake Number Four: He decided to tell her he was attracted to her. Mistake Number Five: He decided to kiss her. Mistake Number Six: He decided not to stop there, and went on to touch her body. Mistake Number Seven: He noticed that he was getting very aroused and decided to keep going . . . And I don't have to spell out the details of Mistake Numbers Eight, Nine, Ten, etc. **Do you get my point? No one forced him to cheat on you. He made the decision to break his marriage vows many times that night.**

Now for his second brilliant statement: "it didn't mean anything." Is that supposed to make you feel better? He jeopardized his marriage and family, broke your heart, destroyed the trust in the relationship for something that didn't mean anything? *Hey, if it didn't mean anything, then why did he do it in the first place? I'm not sure which is worse, your husband cheating, or his claiming that his infidelity didn't mean any-*

thing and therefore, shouldn't really upset you, a callous attitude which totally disregards all of your feelings.

Perhaps the saddest part of your question comes at the end, when you ask me if you're being old-fashioned for being so upset. I hear the timid voice of a woman who doesn't trust herself, who has allowed herself to be talked out of her feelings ever since she can remember, a woman who is uncomfortable with anger and wishes desperately that this would all just go away. I'll bet you've ignored a lot of issues in your eighteen years of marriage in order to keep the peace, issues that are at the root of your husband's fall from grace. (See Questions 2, 37, 38, 44, and 47—they all apply to your situation.) Deep in your heart, you know you can't ignore this one.

Here's an important point—**since this was a one night stand, not an ongoing affair, and since you've been married for a long time, I don't suggest throwing out your relationship or asking your husband for a divorce right away.** Your relationship is in a serious crisis, but if you are both willing to work hard on honestly communicating about all of your issues, in time I believe you can heal from this incident and go on to build a new, healthier marriage. It's up to you whether you want your husband to move out for an extended period of time, as suggested in Question 70, *but I do suggest you ask him to leave for at least a week, just to give you space and to let him know you mean business.* And you do need to follow the other guidelines regarding a commitment to counseling and healing your marriage.

Remember: your husband's sexual escapade is a warning sign of other problems in the relationship. Now that it got your attention, use it to transform your marriage. There's a wonderful saying: *"Out of every crisis comes a chance to be reborn."*

➤❤❤❤➤ SEE ALSO QUESTIONS 2, 37,
              38, 44, 47, AND 70

73 *Should you continue an affair with a married man who won't leave his wife?*

For three years I've been having a wonderful, loving relationship with a caring and sensitive man. He is everything I've ever wanted, but there's one problem—he's married. He says he doesn't love his wife anymore, but can't leave because of the children, who are four and seven years old. My friends think I'm crazy to put up with this, but I know in my heart that he feels more married to me than to her, and I'm willing to wait. What do you think?

➤━❤❤➤ What do I think? I think your friends are right. I think you're kidding yourself. I think you're settling for someone else's leftovers. I think you're going to wake up one day feeling used, ripped off, and betrayed.

You say this man is everything you've ever wanted, but you are forgetting one important qualification—*he isn't available. I don't care what he tells you or what you want to believe. The reality is, he is married to and living with someone else, and doesn't intend to leave. Do you get it? He isn't yours.* (See Question 24 for why you would choose unavailable men and what "available" means. It's no accident that you ended up with a married man.)

As for your fantasy that he is married to you "in his heart," that's a bunch of you know what. Look around . . . do you see him living with you? Do you hear him introducing you to people as his beloved?

Are you wearing his wedding ring on your finger?
Do you recall him spending Thanksgiving, Christ-
mas, and New Year's with you? No, because "in his
heart," he's right where he decided to be—with his
wife and children. I'm not saying he doesn't love
you. He probably does. I'm not saying he doesn't fantasize about leaving everything for you. I'm sure
that's something he struggles with. *But the bottom line
is that you are his mistress, not his wife.*

Any woman having an affair with a married
man with children needs to realize one thing: **you are
making it so easy for these guys to have their cake
and eat it too**—why should they mess up a good
thing and leave their wives and kids? After all, this
way they get to have sex with two women (don't believe it when he insists they're not doing it anymore—they are!); they get to avoid breaking their
children's hearts; they get to look like the good family man to their friends and relatives and elude the
disapproval divorce would bring; they get to avoid
paying alimony and child support; they get to stay in
their comfortable home instead of moving into a tiny
apartment; they get to control the game.

As for your illusion that he's waiting for the kids
to be older, forget it. First it will be, "I can't leave this
year—Jimmy just made Little League." Then, "Sally's
going through a hard time in school this semester,
and a breakup would upset her too much." Then,
"Jimmy's at that age when he wants to be with his

dad all the time . . . a divorce would devastate him."
Then, "Sally's just starting to date. If I leave now,
she'll hate me and hate all men, and it will scar her
for life." Then, "Jimmy's friends have been experi-
menting with drugs. I'm afraid if I leave his mom,
he'll go downhill." Then, "Sally just got engaged. I
can't ruin her happiness with a terrible announcement now." Before you know it, you'll be sixty-five
years old, and your lover will be asking you to just be
patient a little longer, and wait until after the next
grandchild is born!

My advice: **End this relationship now. Do the
honorable thing for yourself, for this man's wife
and family, and yes, even for him.** Do some serious
work on healing the emotional wounds you are carrying that lead you to believe that you don't deserve
all of a man's love. Get back to a state of integrity and
respect with yourself. If this man leaves his wife and
wants to be with you, then you can go forward together. If he doesn't, you will be free to find someone
whom you don't have to share with anyone.

➤❤❤❤➤ *SEE ALSO QUESTION 24*

74 *After your partner has an affair, should you just forgive and forget? How do you learn to trust again?*

My husband had a three-year affair that recently ended after I found a woman's underwear and earring in my bed when I returned home from a trip. He has kept his promise to break off the relationship and seems to be trying to get close to me again. But I'm having a hard time trusting him. He says I should stop punishing him for the past, and just "forgive and forget." Is he right?

➤➤➤ Do you actually need to ask me that question? How are you supposed to forgive and forget your husband's three-year affair, carried on in your own bed, no less, as if it were a small transgression like forgetting to take out the trash? Does he actually expect to get away with not having to be accountable at all for what happened? Three years isn't a one night stand, which is hurtful enough. Three years is a relationship. Pretty hard to just block it out of your mind.

Let me ask you something: Why should you trust your husband after what he did to you? Do you have any reason to believe he has gone through a major emotional transformation and is a different person? Do you have any evidence that he has experienced a personality change, and isn't the same type of guy who screwed another woman behind your back for three years? Has he been in serious recovery,

or found God? What has he done, other than stop
sleeping with his mistress, to repair the wounds in
the relationship? From what you've said, not much.

Here's what I have to say to people who cheat
and then accuse their partner of not trusting them:
*You're the one who betrayed your partner. You're the
one who broke the trust. It's not her responsibility to
learn to trust you again. It's your job to earn back
her trust.* This is my response to your husband, and
his claim that you are punishing him by not trusting
him. You're not punishing him, you're just being realistic.

As for this "forgive and forget" philosophy,
here's something to think about. If you are very for-
tunate, and your husband is willing to go through a
major personal transformation profound enough to
demonstrate that he isn't the same person who
cheated on you, you may be able to build a new marriage based on new values. **If this happens, I believe
that in time, you will forgive your husband for
what he did to you. But you will never, never forget.**

(Don't forget to read Question 70 and follow the
guidelines I've described.)

➤♥♥♥➤   SEE ALSO QUESTION 70

75

Is it acceptable for a cheating partner to still see the person she cheated with after the affair is over?

Six months ago, I found out that my girlfriend was having an affair with one of her business associates. We broke up temporarily, but have since gotten back together and our relationship is much better. The problem I'm having is that she still does a lot of business with this guy and sees him quite often. She claims there is nothing between them anymore, but I feel very uncomfortable with the whole situation. Am I overreacting?

➤♥♥➤ I don't believe you're overreacting at all. I'd be pretty disturbed if my partner were still seeing someone with whom he'd had an affair. I don't care how sincere your girlfriend is—*every time she sees the guy she slept with, she's going to have flashbacks of their relationship, and it makes it that much more difficult to let go of the past and go forward.* Recovering alcoholics don't hang out at liquor stores. They know better. For this same reason, your girlfriend shouldn't be hanging around her ex-lover, especially so soon after the affair.

On a positive note, you both did the right thing in breaking up temporarily, and then starting over. And if you're working on your relationship, it has a good chance of surviving. You're already noticing that things are better, and that's a good sign.

It's really important to make a clean break from some-

one with whom you're trying to end a relationship, and even more essential when that relationship was an illicit affair. I understand that your girlfriend works with this guy, but there has to be a way she can avoid contact with him. Talk with her about your concerns. Make sure you don't sound like you're accusing her of anything, or even not trusting her to be faithful. Instead, share your feelings about the situation, and ask her if she'd be more comfortable not seeing him. Perhaps you can come up with some options that work for both of you.

76 Is there such a thing as an emotional affair? Is it as bad as a sexual affair?

I'm a married man of twelve years who's been having what you might call an emotional affair with a friend for the past several years. She is also married, and although we've never had sex, there is a very intense attraction between us. We talk on the phone every day, have lunch a few times a week, and feel very close. I love my wife, but we are very different people, and don't share a lot of the same interests and attitudes. I don't want to get divorced because it would hurt my wife, although my "friend" says she would leave her husband for me. Does this "count" as an affair, even though we haven't done anything?

➡️❤️❤️➡️ You know it counts, or you wouldn't be asking me about it. There are many ways to be intimate with another person, and sex is only one of them. *You are having a very intimate relationship with another woman while you are married, and that definitely qualifies as an emotional affair.* How are you cheating on your wife if you're not sleeping with this woman? **You are sharing feelings and experiences with her that a person should only share with his intimate partner.** Imagine telling your wife, *"I'm madly in love with another woman. I think about her day and night. We are best friends, and I count the minutes until I can see her."* Your wife asks "Have you had sex with her?" When you respond "No," do you actually believe your wife would say, "Oh well, then, there's no problem"?

I'll be honest with you—it sounds like your marriage has been over for a long time, and that you and your wife have become roommates. You aren't really in a marriage at all; you're involved in a living arrangement. You're being dishonest with your wife, your children, and most of all, yourself. If you told me you were having a sexual affair with someone you didn't want to ultimately be with, I'd tell you to end the affair and work on your marriage. But it appears that you have truly created a deeply meaningful relationship with this other person, and that you are more compatible with her than with your own wife.

You are experiencing what I call "The Divided Path," the moment when you realize that the single path you and your mate traveled on for many years has split into two, each going in a different direction. You have grown apart, not because of suppressed emotional issues, but because your own personal growth has led you to two different places, two different sets of interests and values. There may still be a lot of love and caring there, **but for either of you to take the other's path would be a detour from your own destiny.**

For this reason, I believe it's time to end your marriage. Believe me, your wife feels your emotional absence, whether you talk about it or not. She can't have been happy these past few years either and must experience her own kind of loneliness and isolation. *If she's not what you want, then you're not what she wants either. You are doing her a disservice by remaining in the relationship physically while your mind, heart, and spirit are elsewhere.* This isn't about you leaving her for someone else. It's about you leaving for you. **And remember, freeing your partner to find someone who will truly love and accept her just the way she is is an act of great love.**

I'm in a terrible situation. I'm married to a man I've loved since I was a teenager, but I am having an affair with some-one I met at night school. I know I need to choose between them, but the truth is, I feel like I am in love with both of them and don't know what to do. They are opposites in every way, and each has qualities the other is missing, so it's hard for me to even compare them. Is it possible to love two people? Is there a way out of this dilemma for me?

Oh yes, it's certainly possible to love two people at the same time. In fact it's possible (though complicated and not recommended) to love many people at once. The human heart knows no bounds to the love it can feel and express, and if you allow yourself to see the beauty and uniqueness in-side of someone, and there's enough chemistry and compatibility there, you could easily fall in love. *The problem is that it's hard enough to make an intimate rela-tionship with one person work, let alone handle two!* I see from your question that you're already discovering this for yourself.

One thing is clear—you can't go on the way you have been, married and yet having a love affair with someone else. **You are being terribly unfair to both partners, and, to be blunt, staying involved with them both while you decide which you want is pure selfishness.** You shouldn't have gotten involved with your lover in the first place—you're married. And that's where your commitment and obligation must lie.

To you, and to anyone who's cheating on your partner with someone you also love, here's what I strongly recommend:

IF YOU'RE CHEATING:

1. *End the relationship with your secret lover immediately.* Cut off all forms of contact with him, and let him know you are going to give your marriage 100 percent in order to make a decision to stay or to leave.

2. *Return, at least temporarily, to the commitment of your marriage. You must be sure you have done everything you can to make it work.* Whether you tell your mate about the affair is up to you, although I believe holding back the truth always destroys true intimacy. But you must give the relationship every opportunity to succeed, taking into account all of the information in earlier parts of this book (see Questions 2, 3, 7, 12, 26, 37, 38). *Until you and your partner acknowledge that your marriage is in trouble and get help to heal it, you won't know for sure if your husband is the right one for you or not.* Besides, what chance does he

have to make you happy while you are secretly comparing him to this other guy?

3. *If you have tried everything and still feel your
   husband is not right for you, then it's time to
   leave. However, your leaving has to be independent of whether or not you think Guy #2 is who
   you want. **If you have doubts about him, it's
   not fair to stay with your husband just in
   case your affair doesn't work out!** Your* decision about continuing or ending your marriage should have nothing to do with how
   well the affair is going. That's why you need
   to stop the affair first, and then decide.

➤❤❤❤➤ *SEE ALSO QUESTIONS 2, 3,
            7, 12, 26, 37, AND 38*

78 Should you trust someone with a history of infidelity?

I'm in a new relationship with a great guy. We're both divorced, so we have a lot in common and really want to work on the relationship. My problem is that he cheated on his ex-wife several times during their marriage. He doesn't defend what he did and says he has learned a lot since then, and would never be unfaithful in a relationship again. Should I trust him? Is there a greater chance that he will cheat on me since he's already done it before?

➤♥♥♥➤ There are people in the world for whom being sexually faithful is next to impossible. Then, there are others who get themselves into an unfulfilling relationship once in their life, and try to dull the pain of disappointment with an affair. If you told me your boyfriend has a history of cheating on every girlfriend or wife in his past, I'd tell you to run in the other direction as quickly as possible. But your story is quite different. This sounds like a man who was in an unhappy relationship, couldn't bring himself to leave, and made the mistake of having affairs. *So it's possible that both his divorce and his infidelity have taught him a lot about himself and relationships that he never knew before, and that he actually is a better person because of those painful yet eye-opening experiences.*

If your boyfriend has truly undergone a personal transformation since his divorce, he's actually less likely to cheat on you because he tried it and

knows what a nightmare infidelity is. However, if he hasn't done any significant work on himself, it is possible that the emotional programming which prompted him to cheat once could activate that behavior again. Your job is to determine whether or not he has truly seen the light. Go over Questions 10, 12, and 26 with him. They will help assess how committed he is to understanding himself and what he has learned since his divorce. Be honest about your concerns; make sure you're getting what you need, and take it one day at a time.

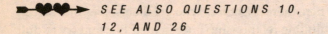 *SEE ALSO QUESTIONS 10, 12, AND 26*

Breaking Up,
Starting Over

My girlfriend broke up with me a few months ago because she said she wanted to date other people and needed some space. I still love her very much. How can I get her back?

➤❤❤➤ You can't. Your former girlfriend obviously doesn't want to be with you right now. She's not interested. She's made that very clear. So as much as it hurts, and I know it does, you have to let go. *You say you love her very much. Fine—then support her quest for happiness, even though it doesn't involve you, and honor her wishes to not be with you.* As difficult as this sounds, what are your true alternatives? There are none.

Let's talk about you for a moment. You're in love with someone who has rejected you, and are having a hard time getting over her. It's no accident that you're in this situation, and I'll bet it isn't the first time you've loved someone more than she has loved you. Please use this time alone to do some serious emotional work on yourself (see Questions 12, 15, and 24). You're acting out a painful pattern, and even though you believe your troubles would be over if only your girlfriend would come back, that's not the answer. **You need to heal that insecure little boy inside you that doesn't believe he's lovable and thinks he has to work really hard to get someone to**

care about him. Don't make your goal getting her back—make it getting yourself back.

━❤❤❤━►   S E E   A L S O   Q U E S T I O N S   1 2 ,
                 1 5 ,   A N D   2 4

80 *How long should it take to recover from a breakup?*

My boyfriend and I were together for six years and recently ended our relationship. Although I feel it was for the best, I still miss him terribly and can't seem to stop crying. Does this mean I made a mistake? It's been almost five weeks. How long will it take me to get over him?

▶━💚💚━▶ Anyone who's ever ended a relationship with someone they loved, and perhaps still love very much, can certainly relate to how you are feeling. One of the most difficult parts of breaking up is getting through that first layer of sadness and loss without doubting your decision. Don't misinterpret the pain you're feeling as a sign that you did something wrong when you ended your relationship. It's a natural part of the healing process.

I've found that breaking up involves four inevitable stages of recovery. Together, these stages take approximately one to two years to complete, although, of course, the length of time will be less if you were in a brief relationship. In your case, you spent six years with your boyfriend, so you will probably take a while to completely heal. Here's a brief description of the four stages:

STAGE ONE: **The Tearing Apart**
DURATION: **Two Weeks to Two Months**

When you love another person, you merge your hopes, your dreams, your energies, and your heart with that person's. When you end the relationship, you go through a process I call the *Tearing Apart*, because that is how it feels, doesn't it? . . . like a part of you is being torn away. Even if you want that familiar person out of your life, you will still experience this phase, *and the longer you have been together, the longer the Tearing Apart will last.*

In this phase you may cry a lot, feel lost, hopeless or alone, lose your appetite, and even feel a constant pain or ache in your heart. You might notice that you are swamped with painful memories, and find it difficult to get through each day. During the Tearing Apart, it's natural to worry that you'll never be happy again, to feel sorry for yourself, and of course, be tempted to return to your partner.

The Tearing Apart is the hardest part of breaking up. It feels like it will never end—but it will. You can speed up the process by doing the following:

1. *Let yourself cry and mourn as much as possible.* The more you try to hold it in, the longer it will last.

2. *Keep busy and spend time with friends and family.* Schedule yourself in advance so you don't find yourself sitting home alone and feeling miserable. Don't forget, however, to also spend quiet time doing some emotional work so you don't carry the same love habits into the next relationship.

3. *Take good care of your body.* The better you feel physically, the more psychologically stable you will be. *That means avoid the temptation to numb yourself with drugs, alcohol, and heavy doses of sugar.* They will only add to your sensitivity and depression.

4. *Avoid seeing or talking with your former partner. No matter how tempted you are to call or see your ex when you're feeling lonely, don't do it!* The more you stay connected, the longer this stage of your recovery will take.

STAGE TWO: **The Adjustment**
DURATION: **Two to Six Months**

You know you've entered Stage Two when you actually start feeling good for a few days at a time! The most intense pain of the Tearing Apart is over. Now it is time to adjust to your new life without your partner. You begin to re-form your personality and identity as a single person, start bonding with other people, get your life back in order, and look ahead to the future.

During The Adjustment, you will be able to talk or think about your partner without feeling you will fall apart or become angry. You no longer feel like a victim, and you will cry or feel sad less frequently— maybe once or twice a week instead of every day! You will start having fun again, and even begin noticing attractive people you'd like to meet. You'll also have a much clearer perspective on what went wrong in the relationship, which will give you a sense of hope about the future.

STAGE THREE: **Healing**
DURATION: **Six Months to One Year**

Stage Three sees your life becoming normal again. You no longer feel as if you are in transition. You may be involved in a new relationship, or interested in beginning one. You will have much of your business with your former partner settled, or on the way to being settled in the case of divorce. You're healing the wounds and becoming whole again. *You have survived!*

In this stage, you can talk with and about your former partner without getting upset, and even feel positive about the rightness of what has happened. You feel and look better than you have in a while, and have a sense of enthusiasm about your future.

Your sadness or nostalgia for your ex-lover may surface once every week or so, but passes quickly.

| STAGE FOUR: | **Recovery** |
| DURATION: | **One to Two Years** |

Stage Four is a transitional stage in which you clear out any remaining pain from the relationship you've ended, and firmly establish yourself in your new life. You no longer think of yourself as having just ended a relationship. By now, you have a new social structure around you—new friends, new love interests, new directions.

In this stage, you have hopefully adopted new habits and ways of behaving as a result of the mistakes you made in the previous relationship, and are ready to love and be loved again. People no longer ask you how you're doing in sympathetic voices! Your new life has begun. Enjoy it!

You can take one year or five years to go through these four stages. It all depends on how willing you are to let go of the past, work through all your feelings for the purpose of healing them, and receive the lessons from your experience. Take one day at a time, and before you know it, you *will* be loved again.

I'm recovering from a very dysfunctional relationship in which my husband lied, cheated, and used me for my money. I knew inside that he wasn't good for me from the beginning, but it took me eight years to get up the courage to leave. My life is finally back in order, but I'm scared to death to start dating, let alone fall in love. How can I learn to trust love and men again after what happened?

➤ 💕💕 ➤ *It's not men whom you need to learn to trust again—it's yourself.* You're the one who chose him; you're the one who allowed him to mistreat you, and looked the other way; you're the one who didn't stand up for yourself; you're the one who didn't listen to that little voice, that little girl inside of you who was screaming *"Don't let him do this to us! He's hurting us! Make him go away!"* And so that's why the person who you need to heal is you.

Each time you give your power away to a man by allowing him to treat you disrespectfully or unlovingly, you lose respect and love for yourself. This is what's happened to you—*you were in a negative self-esteem cycle.* You allowed your husband to get away with mistreating you, you didn't stick up for yourself, and this resulted in your feeling upset, depressed, and bad about yourself. When you felt bad about yourself, your self-confidence decreased. And when your self-confidence was low, the next time he mistreated you, you had even less courage to stand up for yourself, and the cycle repeated itself over and over.

Do you see my point? Love didn't hurt you—*you* hurt you by mistaking the dysfunctional relationship you had for love. I know that you think of yourself as a victim, but I have a saying: *"It takes two people to create an accident—one to drive the truck and the other to lie down in the road and say 'it's okay to run me over.'"* **You gave your power away to this man. It's time to take it back. You've already taken the first step—leaving—and the second step is acknowledging that *you* gave him the power to hurt you.**

See Questions 10, 12, and 15 to learn more about why you chose this kind of partner, and how you can learn from your mistakes by making a *Relationship Mistake List and Relationship Rule Book. The more conscious you become of all the unhealthy mini-decisions you made during your marriage, the more you will realize that the painful events didn't just happen to you and are therefore preventable ... but only if you commit yourself to paying attention and taking charge of your love life!*

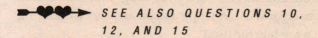 **SEE ALSO QUESTIONS 10, 12, AND 15**

82 When is it too late to leave a loveless relationship and find happiness?

I've been married for thirty-two years to a man who doesn't give me any of the love or affection I need. We were married in our early twenties, but never had much in common, and we live politely and passionlessly together. I've finally admitted to myself that I am miserable, but I'm afraid to leave after all these years—besides, our children and friends would be shocked. Am I just being selfish, or is it too late for me to find happiness?

Too late? Of course it's not too late. As long as you are alive, you have the opportunity to experience love. I can't tell you how many stories I've heard about men and women in their sixties, seventies, even eighties meeting someone just right for them and falling in love. You deserve to be happy, and just because you have sacrificed your own joy for the sake of your family for years doesn't mean that you need to continue that way until you die. As for your friends and children being shocked, they'd be even more shocked if you confessed that you have been miserable all this time, but felt you were doomed to suffer. And by the way, your husband is probably just as unhappy as you are, and wondering if it's too late for him!

You're what I call "love-starved." Your heart is hungry for love that you've imagined, but haven't felt for most, if not all, of your life. **You've probably spent** years doing what you thought was right, but never asking yourself if it was right for you. Now, as you look back on the life you've been living, it seems empty and devoid of all meaning. And although it may appear that this realization is a terrible thing, I believe that it is actually the beginning of your emotional and spiritual rebirth.

Find the courage to follow your heart. You'll need to do some serious work on yourself in order to understand how you could have lived in so much denial for all these years. (See Questions 12 and 15.) Reach out to others for support. Believe me, you aren't the first woman who's woken up from a deep sleep in her later years and had the guts to honor her feelings. There are many just like you out there who will be overjoyed to help you cross over from the empty life you've been leading into one that is vibrant, meaningful, and yes, even happy!

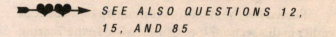 *SEE ALSO QUESTIONS 12, 15, AND 85*

83 Should you continue to spend time with an ex-lover as a friend after you break up?

After four years of dating, my boyfriend and I mutually agreed it would be best for us to break up. However, we still spend a lot of time together, going out to eat, seeing movies, and we talk on the phone almost every day. Now I'm starting to date someone new, and he told me it bothers him that I am so close with my ex, but my ex is still my best friend. What should I do?

→♥♥♥→ Hmmmm, let's see, why in the world would your new boyfriend find it upsetting that your former lover is your "best friend"? Why would it bother him that you talk with your ex every day, spend time with him, and do everything you used to do but sleep with him? *Why would your new boyfriend react this way? Because he is playing fair and you're not! Because you are being incredibly insensitive and selfish, not just in regard to his feelings, but to your former boyfriend's feelings as well.* (See Question 30.)

Remember the stages of breaking up I spoke about earlier in this section? (See Question 80.) **In the Tearing Apart, the first stage of letting go, it's essential to create as much emotional and physical space between you and your former partner as possible.** This allows your heart to feel the vacuum made by the loss of your lover, and even though it will hurt, it is this vacuum that will create the opening for new love to find a home inside you. *Your new boyfriend cannot become a part of you* *if the space in your heart is already occupied, and this is exactly what's happening.*

Several things are possible: Perhaps you moved on to a new relationship too soon, and need to do more emotional work and personal healing before you get involved again; or, it may be that you are so afraid of not being loved that you're hanging on to your former boyfriend until you're absolutely sure that this new relationship will work out. It's as if you are clinging to a life raft until you are certain that the new boat won't sink. *The problem is that until you let go, you won't give this new relationship a chance.* And in the process, you are holding up your former lover's healing process by not allowing him to detach from you.

Let him go. Say good-bye completely, and then spend some time alone in true mourning for the dreams you didn't fulfill together. Then, when you feel ready to be 100 percent present, begin your relationship again with your new partner. Perhaps at some point in the future (not next month!!), when you are totally committed to this or another relationship, you will be able to invite your former boyfriend back into your life as a friend. And trust that ahead of you lies more love and happiness than you have ever known before.

SEE ALSO QUESTIONS 29, 30, AND 80

84

How can you break up with someone without causing that person pain?

I've known for a while that I need to break up with my girl-friend, but I keep putting it off for one reason—I feel so guilty about hurting her. She wants to stay in the relationship and will be devastated when I leave. How can I break up with her so that I don't cause her emotional pain?

➡❤❤❤➡ *YOU CAN'T.* It's that simple. That's like asking "how can I go swimming without getting wet?," or "how can I chop this onion without break-ing the skin?" You can't. And if you're planning to wait until you feel you aren't going to hurt your girl-friend, you might as well marry her now, because that day will never come. When you tell her you are leaving, it will hurt her. When you walk out the door, it will hurt her. *But remember this: it will hurt her much more if you lead her on for another month, an-other year, or commit to her out of guilt, only to fi-nally confess at some point, that "I always knew I should have broken up with you." It will hurt her much more to stay in a relationship with a man who isn't fully emotionally present, a man who can't give her the complete commitment she deserves.*

Let me say something that may shock you— *you're not staying to avoid hurting her. You're staying to avoid feeling bad about yourself.* You can't stand the idea of being the "bad guy," the "heart-breaker"; you can't tolerate the thought of living with guilt. *And so even though it appears that you are protecting her from pain, you are really protecting yourself.* (See Question 30.)

Whenever I hear this kind of story, I know I am speaking to a bona fide rescuer, whose identity and self-esteem are tied in with making sure you are never the cause of pain to someone you love. (See Question 21.) You see, it is your girlfriend's pain that both attracted you, and now, is trapping you. In the beginning, you were captivated by it, hoping that you would be able to heal her hurt and "save" her, thus proving to yourself that you are good enough. *Now that you realize you cannot love her as she should be loved, it is again her pain that is torturing you by triggering your own pain (which has always been the real issue), for you cannot leave without feeling you are a failure.*

Release your girlfriend now. Release her so she can find a man who will truly love and accept her as she is. Don't wait another day. And then turn toward yourself and search deep in your own heart for that wounded little boy that couldn't make Mommy happy, or couldn't save Daddy from despair, and do what you've been needing to do all along—rescue him.

➤❤❤❤➤ *SEE ALSO QUESTIONS 21 AND 30*

85

How do you know when a relationship just isn't going to work, and it's time to leave?

►❤❤❤► One of the most painful things in life is admitting to yourself that the relationship you're in isn't working, and that it's time to leave. You wish you could go to sleep, wake up the next morning and have everything be different, but you can't. You wish your partner would magically become the person you want him to be, but he won't. You know you've put off making the decision long enough, and that it's time to say good-bye.

I believe that you should do everything in your power to salvage a troubled relationship. That includes using all possible sources of outside help including *professional counseling, seminars, books, support groups, recovery programs, etc.* However, you may reach a point at which you feel you cannot or do not want to continue with your partner, and at that point, you need to make the decision to stay or go.

It's time to end your relationship when:

- **You realize you are incompatible.** In my book *Are You the One for Me?* I explained why *"love is not enough to make a relationship work."* You need compatibility. You have to like your partner as much as you love him! (See Question 17 and *Are You the One for Me?*) When you are not compatible with your mate, your love won't be enough to overcome your problems.

Only when you have found a new, compatible relationship will you realize how right you were to leave the incompatible one behind.

- **You realize you have no sexual chemistry between you.** If you recognize that you and your partner don't have enough chemistry to make your love more than a good friendship, you need to set both yourself and your partner free to find a complete union with a more suitable mate. Remember, however, that if the chemistry has temporarily disappeared, you need to first do everything you can to heal the relationship before deciding to leave. (See Questions 2, 7, 13, 47, and 58.)

- **You and your partner have grown in two different directions.** I strongly believe that we often come together with a mate for a certain length of time in order to be each other's teachers, and when we have learned the necessary lessons, we need to go on. You and your partner may have grown tremendously in your years together and given each other great emotional gifts. *However, you may have arrived at what I call the Divided Path, a point at which you are destined to travel in different directions.* When your goals and styles of growing are too different, it will no longer be healthy or emotionally fulfilling for you to live together. (See Question 76.)

- **The hardest part about reaching the Divided Path is that your love for your partner may not have changed, and that makes it even more difficult to say good-bye.** I know, because I've arrived at the Divided Path several times in my life. All I can say to reassure you is that each time my new path brought me greater happiness, wisdom, and love than I had ever known before.

- **Your partner has a Fatal Flaw he will not deal with.** There are millions of men and women who have had the heartbreaking experience of having to leave someone they loved because that person refused to face his own Fatal Flaws, whether it's alcoholism, drug abuse, addiction to pornography, or rage. (See Questions 23 and 25.) *If your partner will not seek help in battling his problem, or is in total denial that he even has a problem, you have no healthy choice but to end the relationship.*

- **Your partner refuses to work on your relationship.** This is perhaps the saddest reason of all you may have to end a partnership, and the biggest waste. *If your partner refuses to face or discuss your problems, and will not agree to any outside help in solving your conflicts, he has broken his commitment to your relationship* as much as if he had an affair. He may be scared; he may have had an abusive childhood; he may have a wonderful, loving heart somewhere inside of him. *The fact remains that, unless he is willing to be an active participant in your partnership, there is no partnership, and you must leave.* (See Questions 14 and 37.)

If you are presently struggling with making the painful decision of whether to stay or leave, I hope this helps you to feel more certain about your choice and gives you confidence that, although it's not easy, you're doing the right thing.

SEE ALSO QUESTIONS 2, 7, 13, 14, 17, 23, 25, 37, 47, 58, AND 76

86 *Should you stay in an unhappy marriage for the sake of your children?*

I married my wife because she got pregnant with our first child after we'd been dating for two months, and I felt it was the right thing to do. Since then, we've had two more children, and live a good life, but the truth is, I've never loved her. For eight years, I've been sacrificing my happiness for one reason—my kids. I would never do anything to hurt them, but I don't know how much longer I can go on like this. Should I stay married for the sake of my children, even though I'm miserable?

━━♥♥♥━━ The most painful and difficult issue to consider when thinking of ending a marriage is always the children. No parent wants to be a source of unhappiness to their children, whom they love more than life itself, and therefore the guilt that accompanies discussions about breaking up can be devastating. The answer I'm going to give you to your question is based on almost two decades of my experience working with tens of thousands of people, and although some professionals or clergy may disagree, it's an answer I feel very strongly about. *Never stay in an unhappy relationship for the sake of your children. Your personal unhappiness will have a much more damaging effect on your children than your divorce ever could.*

Children want to see their parents happy. They feel responsible for making their parents happy, and believe me, they know when you aren't, no matter how good you think you are at hiding the truth from them. If you stay in an unhappy marriage for the sake of your children, I believe you will be causing them more emotional harm than if you divorced. They will feel responsible for your sacrifice, and this puts tremendous pressure on a child. *"I stayed for your sake" is no favor.*

I have worked with thousands of grown-up "children" in my seminars and found the following to be true: *The children whose parents divorced and found love and happiness, either alone or with new partners, grow up feeling good about themselves and their parents. They have a healthy attitude toward love and relationships because they had positive role models for loving themselves and making love work.*

In contrast, some of the most unhappy people I have worked with are grown-ups whose parents stayed together in passionless, dead relationships, colored with suppressed anger and resentment. These men and women develop a mistrust of love and relationships, as well as an inability to express love or feel worthy of receiving it—all because they had negative role models for making love work. The bottom line is: IF YOUR CHILDREN SEE YOU BEING WELL LOVED, THEY WILL FEEL LOVABLE AND HOPEFUL ABOUT HAVING A WONDERFUL RELATIONSHIP. IF YOUR CHILDREN SEE YOU BEING UNLOVED, THEY WILL FEEL UNLOVABLE AND

PESSIMISTIC ABOUT HAVING A WONDERFUL RELATIONSHIP.

My own parents stayed together for many years "for the sake of the children" before finally divorcing when I was eleven. In my emotional healing work, I have discovered something that recent research also concludes: *the most pain was not from the actual divorce or the years that followed, but from the eleven years prior to that when I lived with two unhappy people.* I felt responsible for not being able to make them happy, and unconsciously formed a belief that *love = pain, fear, and unfulfilled longing.* (See Question 15.) The emotional scars from their marriage took me many, many years to heal, and it was only after several of my own failed relationships and intensive emotional work that I was able to find and maintain a healthy, loving relationship with a man.

I have never met a grown-up child whose parents stayed unhappily together who felt the following sentiment: *"Mom and Dad, I want you to know that even though you have been in a passionless, miserable relationship for forty years that has left you emotionally numb and drained, I really appreciate your sacrifice. I'm glad I can say 'my parents are still married,' and don't really care if you're happy or not, as long as I have my fantasy that your marriage worked."* On the contrary, when I ask my audiences how many of them, now that they are adults, wish their parents had gotten divorced, over half of the people raise their hands!! Of course, if you ask your young children how they would feel if Mommy and Daddy split up, they will tell you to stay together. It won't be until they have their own relationships as adults that they will look upon yours with new eyes, suddenly realize how unhappy you truly were, and feel grief for all you gave up.

Your job as a parent is to know what's best for your child, whether or not your child agrees with your decision. When your little girl asks if she can eat ice cream for dinner, and you respond "No!" she may cry and claim that you are mean. Because you know that ice cream doesn't comprise a healthy meal, you are able to stick to your decision in spite of her tears. In your heart, you know you are making this decision for her own good.

This is the same attitude you must have when deciding the future of your relationship. Yes, your children will cry when you tell them you are getting divorced, just as I did when my parents told me. *But as they grow older and learn to see you as people, and not just parents, they will develop compassion for your situation and understanding about your decision.* They will realize that you were not just doing it for your own good, but for theirs as well.

You owe it to your children to work very hard on your marriage, and do everything you can to make it work. But if you come to the point where you realize that the marriage cannot work, then you owe it to your children to separate from your partner, and free

yourself to find the love you deserve, and the rela-
tionship they can one day look up to.

SEE ALSO QUESTIONS 12
AND 15

87 Is there such a thing as having been hurt too much to even want to give a relationship one more chance?

For twenty years, I tried to get my husband to give to me and the relationship, with no success. He is one of those people who just shuts you out if he doesn't want to hear what you have to say, and he refused to even discuss my needs for love, communication, or affection. I fought my urge to leave him in order to keep our family together, and stayed, living a lonely, miserable existence. Finally, I've gotten up the courage to go, and all of a sudden, he's woken up, and is acting like a new person. He's started therapy; he writes me love notes; he holds my hands and cries, begging me to give him another chance. He's doing everything I ever wanted, but my heart is closed, and I feel nothing. Can a person be hurt so much that you just don't want to try one more time?

━━♥♥♥► What you're describing is one of the saddest patterns I hear about in relationships: *the partner whose love has died from years of neglect, only to discover when she decides to leave that her husband finally gets everything she's been trying to tell him for years . . . and it's too late.* I do believe that there is a point of "no return" in some relationships, when you've experienced so much hurt, disappointment, and rejection that you can no longer feel anything for your partner.

It takes years to get to this point—years of repressing your feelings, years of ignoring your needs,

years of telling yourself you'll try just one more time
to make it work. Finally, your heart closes to your
mate for good. Like a bank account that has experienced only withdrawals and no deposits, you are left
with a zero balance. So when he finally shows up and
asks for what you have, you truly have nothing to
give. (See Questions 2, 7, 38, and 47 for more insight.)

You know this in your heart, but like most
women, it goes against your nature to say "No" to a
man when he asks for your love, patience, and commitment, and so you're feeling guilty rejecting him,
aren't you? Well, don't. He rejected you for many,
many years. *This is his karma, the result of his attitude
and actions toward you and the marriage. Over and over
again, he chose not to heed your warnings, not to answer
your pleas, not to reach back when you reached out in need.
Now, it's your turn to choose, and you are making the
right choice in leaving.*

Go forward in your life, knowing that you did
the best you could, knowing that you waited until
you couldn't wait anymore, and knowing that loving
yourself enough to finally leave is an important spiritual victory.

*SEE ALSO QUESTIONS 2, 7,
38, AND 47*

►❤❤► It all depends on circumstances sur-rounding your divorce. *The more wounded, angry, or victimized you feel about your breakup, the longer you need to wait before even thinking of getting involved again.* If your relationship ended very badly or sud-denly, you will need more time than if the breakup was mutual and long overdue. If you have children, you will probably need more time to stabilize the family than if you and your mate didn't have kids. If there was infidelity, you will definitely need a longer healing period than if the marriage ended amicably. Understanding the four stages of recovery men-tioned earlier in this section will also help you iden-tify where you are in your postrelationship process, and therefore, when you're ready to get involved again.

A few important cautions: **Don't jump into a new relationship just to fill up the emptiness and avoid facing your pain. Don't fool yourself into thinking your former partner was the problem, and now that you're finished with him or her, all you need to do is find someone else. Remember—you chose that person. Find out why before you choose someone else.** (See Questions 12 and 15.) And after reading through this book, I'm sure you know that I am going to tell you that you need to do some deep emotional work on both understanding and healing your past, as well as getting clear on how to avoid making mistakes in the future. (See Questions 10, 25, and 26.)

Now, it's possible that in spite of everything I've said, the Universe will suddenly deliver a wonderful new partner into your life very soon after your breakup, and in the midst of your healing process. Please—if you find yourself falling in love with a wonderful person who is committed to his growth and supportive of yours, who acknowledges your need to heal, and who is everything you've ever wanted, **don't say** *"Could you come back in about nine months?"* Grab on to him, and thank God for bringing you someone to keep you company during your recovery, and even aid you in the process. Love is a gift and has its own sense of cosmic timing that is often unfathomable.

SEE ALSO QUESTIONS 10,
12, 15, 25, 26, AND 80

89 Is it harmful to continue having sex with your ex-lover?

My boyfriend and I broke up a few months ago, and we both agree that we need to go our separate ways. The problem is that we can't seem to stop having sex. The first time I thought it was just for old times' sake, but now he comes over every weekend and we end up in bed for days. We've always been intensely attracted to one another, and the sex is fantastic. Neither of us has met anyone else, so we're not hurting anyone. Can what we're doing be harmful?

➤➤❤❤❤➤ I'd love to know your definition of "breaking up." Is it when you tell people you are no longer together, even though you're screwing your brains out? *Let's be honest here—you haven't broken up. You've just taken all of the responsibility out of the relationship, all that messy unpleasant stuff like communication about issues, commitment, and confrontation over differences.* What's left is the fun. Only instead of admitting that you're having a relationship with a guy purely for sex, because you can't seem to get along in any other area, you're pretending to be "broken up." That way, you can think of your sexual encounters as random events that just happened to occur, rather than what they truly are.

If you and your boyfriend/ex-boyfriend/ weekend stud or whatever you want to call him want to take responsibility for your lives, have an honest discussion about what's happening. *Either accept the fact that you are using each other for sex, and would like things to remain this way . . . OR, if you truly want a healthy new relationship, stop seeing each other completely and create an opening for a more compatible partner to enter your life.* You can't do both. After all, what are you going to say if you meet some great guy at a party, and he asks if you're available: *"Oh yes, I'm available, except for the nights when I have sex with my ex!"* I don't think so. . . .

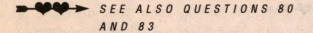 SEE ALSO QUESTIONS 80 AND 83

Living
and
Loving

90 Is it appropriate for a widower or widow to start dating again even if his grown children disapprove?

My wife of forty-two years passed away six months ago after a long illness. We had a wonderful relationship, and the last few years were very painful as I watched her suffer and knew I'd have to let her go. I'm in my late sixties, still working and very active. I recently met a widow through my synagogue and we've begun to date. I enjoy this woman's company very much, and frankly, after almost half a century of marriage, don't see myself living alone. The problem is my children, ages forty and thirty-six and both married—they are appalled that I could possibly feel anything for anyone but their mother, and refuse to even meet this woman. Should I stop seeing her so I don't cause the family pain?

➡️💗💗💗➡️ What a good father you are—thinking about your children's pain, and putting their feelings before yours. My response is: WHAT ABOUT YOUR PAIN? It's easy for your children to be so morally idealistic and sit in judgment of your desire to date when they're waking up in the morning next to their wives and husbands, and going through the day knowing they won't have to come home to an empty house. But what about you? *You're the one who had to care for your dying wife for years. You're the one who is living with loneliness. You're the one whose heart has been broken and is trying to mend.*

You are entitled to live the rest of your life with

happiness. You obviously loved your wife very much, and your marriage left you with a heart full of love, love that wants to be shared, and not packed away in mothballs. It is a credit to your wife that you have so much to give, and feel so positively about partnership, and although this may sound a bit strange, I believe that any new relationship you have will honor her memory. She will always be a part of you, just as your new friend's husband will always be a part of her. **Loving someone new will not take away from your love for your wife—it will be a testimony to how loving your wife was, and how much she taught you.**

Share your feelings with your children, if they will listen, and tell them about the anguish you've suffered for these past few years. Perhaps they only saw you being brave for your wife, and didn't realize what pain you were in. Let them know how lonely you are, and explain that you, too, are getting used to someone else's company. And no matter what their reaction, don't give up this relationship. Who knows, maybe your wife sent her to keep you company?

As for your children, this is what I have to say to them: **Stop being so selfish!** Whose feelings are you worried about when you condemn your father's choices, his or yours? I know you loved your mother, but wanting your father to suffer will not bring her back. You have one parent left. Love him enough to pray for his happiness, and thank God he found someone to offer him comfort and companionship.

91 Is it true that a woman shouldn't pursue a man or initiate a relationship because he will lose interest without the challenge?

A friend of mine told me she read a book that said women should never ask men out, call men, show men they care in the beginning of the relationship or act in an aggressive fashion because it takes away the challenge for a man. What do you think about this advice?

➤♥♥➤ *I THINK IT'S A BUNCH OF BULL!!* It's *disrespectful to men. It's controlling and manipulative, and demeaning to women.* Games are for children, not for grown-ups who want to have healthy, meaningful relationships. The belief that women are so powerless that we somehow need to "trap" a man is sexist, even if it is a woman who espouses this belief. Men aren't animals to be lured and domesticated. They are human beings with the same vulnerabilities and insecurities women have.

It's advice like this that gives women a bad name. This is why some men don't trust us, don't respect us, think of us as superficial, and call us "controlling bitches." They suspect that we behave in a certain way until we've gotten their interest, and then once they're hooked, we drop the demure act and become needy and demanding. How can we blame them for drawing these conclusions when they see a book like the one you mentioned?

I think that deliberately making a man feel rejected or inferior in order to make him pursue you is sick. Would you like to be treated this way? I know I wouldn't. As for the kinds of men who may find this approach exciting because it arouses their primal sense of "the hunt," you are welcome to them, honey. They're power hungry and will always want to keep you in your place.

Now I'm not saying that I think it's perfectly fine to go up to a man at a party and say, *"You have a great butt—let's go back to my place and screw our brains out,"* or to call someone you like five times a day even when he doesn't call you back. That's not owning your power or being an independent woman—it's being obnoxious and insensitive. You don't like it when men treat you in that manner, so what makes you think they would like it any better? But it's ridiculous to pretend you're some quiet little Victorian flower with no feelings of your own, or do a Scarlett O'Hara imitation in the hopes that a man will be intrigued by your mystique. **Be yourself. It's much less exhausting, and in the end, you'll know the man loves you for who you are, not who he thinks you are.**

92 *How soon should a single parent tell a prospective partner that she has children?*

I'm a single mother with two young children. I'm ready to start dating again, but I'm not sure how soon into the relationship I should tell a man I'm interested in that I have kids. I don't want to come on too strong or turn men off.

➤♥♥➤ **Tell him you have children even before you go out on the first date.** What's the point of putting it off? Do you plan to get the guy to really like you, maybe even sleep with him, so that by the time you inform him you are a mother, he won't be able to leave you in spite of how much he dislikes children? *"Waiting" to tell a prospective partner that you are a single mom implies that you feel this is a piece of bad news that you must break to a man gently. Is that how you feel about your kids?* I'm sure it's not. Your children are not a deep, dark secret that you need to hide. They are a wonderful part of your life that makes you the loving, giving person you are, and knowing them will be a gift to anyone.

Are there men who don't want to get involved with a woman with children? Sure there are. Are there men who are so small-minded that they might disqualify you as girlfriend material the moment you bring out the school pictures? You bet. But guess what—if this happens, you will have just saved yourself a tremendous amount of time and heartache by eliminating potential partners who definitely are not right for you. *A man who doesn't want to be with you because you have kids will definitely not be good enough for you or for your children.* Better to find this out before even getting involved, so you don't expose yourself or your children to someone who doesn't fully appreciate you. (In fact, if you're single and childless, you might want to say you have children just to check out a guy's character . . . just kidding, but it's an interesting idea!)

I know you're worried about how your having children can complicate a new relationship, and that's a legitimate concern. Being a parent is a challenge under ordinary circumstances, and even more so when there's the possibility of stepchildren and remarriage. But no couple is without their issues, whether it be his or her kids from a prior relationship, career pressures, health problems, family stress, or just the regular emotional baggage we all carry into relationships. *The right man will fall in love with you as a person and will grow to love your children because they are such a precious part of you.* So when a new guy asks about you, give him a big smile, and proudly whip out those pictures of the kids, saying, "These are two of my greatest assets!"

93 What's your opinion of bachelor parties? Can they have a damaging effect on a relationship?

I need you to settle an argument I'm having with my boyfriend about bachelor parties. He's gone to several since we've been together, and claims they're harmless fun. However, when I make him tell me what goes on there, I can't believe my ears—everything from guys oiling down naked strippers to women putting on a sex show together. The last one he went to, some of the men "participated," if you know what I mean. Every time we talk about this, I get furious, disgusted and turned off for weeks. Should this bother me as much as it does?

➤❤❤➤ You asked for my opinion, so I'll give it to you: *I think that bachelor parties are adolescent, self-indulgent, sexist rituals that are insulting to the bride-to-be, disrespectful of every wife or girlfriend of the men who attend, demeaning to the female "performers," and in general, completely unsupportive of the true spirit of marriage.* Think about it. You're a man about to get married to the woman you love and adore, and the way you prepare for the ceremony is to go out, get completely wasted on booze with your buddies while lusting after naked women other than your bride, being touched, sat on, licked, or even worse. . . . What message is this supposed to give your fiancée? That you can't wait to say "I do"? I don't get it. And believe me, most women who are honest with themselves and you won't either.

In ancient times, the bride and groom would prepare for marriage by going off on vision quests, retreats, going into meditative silence, or undergoing special rituals. I don't think nude mud wrestling at the local strip club qualifies as a spiritual ceremony, do you? *I mean, if men really want to support their friend as he prepares for his wedding, they should sit around together extolling the virtues of his bride, share stories about the benefits of their own committed relationships, and pledge their support to him and his marriage.* I'm sure men reading this will get a big kick out of my suggestion (I can hear you laughing now) but hey . . . guys . . . you're the same ones who five years later are complaining that your wife doesn't want to have sex anymore, and wondering where the passion went. (See Questions 54 and 64.)

You know how you feel about this, so don't apologize for your beliefs to your boyfriend, and don't let him talk you out of your feelings. If after discussing these ideas, your boyfriend still refuses to respect your feelings about his attendance at these thinly veiled excuses for visual, and sometimes physical, orgies, I suggest you seriously reconsider your relationship. Remember: a man's attitude about these kinds of experiences reflects his character. This is someone you're considering to be the possible father of your children, a role model for your sons and an example to your daughters of how

a man should behave toward women. Think about
it. . . .

➤❤❤❤➤   *SEE ALSO QUESTIONS 54*
          AND 64

My boyfriend and I know we need some counseling, but we've had several disappointing experiences with therapists in the past. One man we went to just sat there and let us do all the talking, so we never got any concrete help, and the last counselor we tried gave us long lists of rules for how we should behave and communicate, but never seemed to get to why we were having problems in the first place. How can we make sure we aren't wasting our time, or worse, getting ripped off?

➤━♥♥♥━➤   Be very, very careful when choosing a therapist. *Just as an excellent therapist can help you experience tremendous personal healing, and guide you in creating a strong and healthy relationship, a poor or even mediocre therapist can make your relationship even worse by not dealing with the underlying issues, giving bad advice, or refusing to take a stand against toxic behavior that, if left unidentified, may ultimately destroy your love.* I'm sure I'm going to ruffle some feathers by saying this, but here goes: simply acquiring a degree and license doesn't necessarily mean a person is a "qualified" therapist. They may be according to the laws of their state, but on a personal level they may be inept, lacking in sensitivity, or unable to translate what they've read to the lives of real people.

Part of the problem is that most people don't

know what they should expect to receive from their work with a counselor or therapist. Like you and your friend, they walk into someone's office whom they assume knows more than they do, and accept what happens at face value. So if your therapist just sits there listening and nodding, and once in a while asks *"How did that make you feel?"* or *"What did that bring up for you?"* while you do most of the talking, your session ends, you pay your $75 or $100, and you walk out and think to yourself, "So . . . that's therapy. I guess it takes a long time to make progress." What a joke!! Why not make a tape recording of those questions, listen to it for an hour and save yourself the money!

I'll never forget the person who called my radio show in Los Angeles wondering if his therapy was working. When I asked what went on during the sessions, this gentleman reported that he would talk about his life, his feelings, and his concerns, and then his therapist would ask *"What do you think is going on?"* Then this guy would talk some more until the therapist would repeat his question. "Here's my advice," I told the man. "The next time this therapist asks you what you think is going on, say *'If I knew, I wouldn't be here, would I? You're the therapist. I'm paying you to tell me what's going on.'* "

Imagine that you had terrible stomach pains and went to see your doctor. He asked you to describe your symptoms, and then said "What do you think it is?" and then charged you $150. You'd walk out of the office, wouldn't you? After all, that's why you went to a doctor—he's supposed to figure out what's wrong and help you fix it. *A therapist is supposed to know more than you do about yourself, your relationships, and your emotional patterns. It's his or her job to enlighten you, not your job to do his work for him.*

Here are some guidelines for choosing an effective therapist:

1. **Make sure the relationship you have with your therapist creates the warmth and caring you need to feel safe enough to do the healing you want to do.** Much of the emotional baggage you have came from not feeling loved, cared for, or understood by family or lovers. *Be careful not to choose a therapist who is part of your pattern, and treats you with the same coldness, lack of respect, or indifference as one of your parents or your ex-spouse.* I believe that love is the greatest healer of all and in an atmosphere of love (expressed appropriately of course) you will find it easy to open up and explore the innermost regions of your heart.

2. **Make sure your therapist has done the emotional work you are attempting to do.** The best therapist is the one whose life is dedicated to personal transformation and has been ac-

tively growing and healing himself or herself. It doesn't matter how many books someone has read, research papers he's written, or conferences he's attended—if he's in a continual process of working on himself, he will naturally know how to motivate you, inspire you, be compassionate and help you open the doors in your mind and heart that have been closed. You'd be surprised how many professionals in the mental health field totally avoid processing their own emotions and doing any experiential work whatsoever. *Good therapy isn't about theory—it's a combination of applied understanding and emotional healing. How can someone take you somewhere he's not willing to go?*

3. **Make sure your therapist focuses both on exploring and healing the *causes* of unwanted behavioral and emotional patterns, and on giving you *concrete action steps* you can take in your everyday life to break your unhealthy love habits and discover new, healthier ways of approaching the same old issues.** It's not enough to analyze your past—you need to unlearn behaviors that don't work for you and learn ones that do. A good therapist will give you "homework" to help you integrate your internal breakthroughs with your external life.

4. **Make sure you are experiencing value from sessions with your therapist from the beginning.** It's absurd to believe that you need to wait until you've had ten or twenty sessions with a therapist before you should experience positive results in your life. When people ask me how soon they should expect to experience insight or breakthroughs in therapy, my answer is *"During the first session!"* If you don't hear something valuable, feel something revealing or learn something useful, what is the point of the time and money you are spending?

I'm not suggesting that you should experience miraculous changes in your life or relationship after just one counseling session, but if you don't experience *something* positive that grows with each new appointment, perhaps your therapist is moving too slowly. *Some therapists tend to act like professional babysitters, compassionately listening to your complaints, but never really stretching you to a new level of awareness. And some clients like saying "I'm in therapy," because it looks like they're working on themselves, when in truth, they've chosen a therapist who is more of a confidant than a true healer.* But if you're serious about transformation, find someone who is serious about helping you to transform, NOW.

How do you find a therapist with some of these qualifications? You can find friends or colleagues who have had success with a therapist and ask them for a referral, or call other professionals such as your physician, whom you trust. Ask about the therapist's style and manner, and see if it matches what you're looking for. When you contact the therapist, let him or her know that you want to talk on the phone or in person *before* booking your first appointment, in order to determine whether or not you feel comfortable. Tell the therapist what kind of therapy you're interested in, i.e., someone who will push you, someone who will give you homework, someone who won't just sit there, etc. *Don't be shy about asking questions, and listen carefully to the answers you receive.* You'll know if this person feels right or not. During your first session, reiterate your needs, and remember—it's your session and your money. ASK FOR WHAT YOU NEED.

Finally, remember that a therapist cannot solve your problems for you or heal you or your pain. Only you can heal yourself. Your therapist can be a loving guide who can help you travel through your own emotional jungles in safety and can show you the road to personal freedom.

95 *If you have a friend who is in an abusive relationship, should you try to help, or mind your own business?*

I have a situation that's tearing me apart. My best friend from high school is in a terrible marriage to a real jerk. She's admitted to me that he abuses her verbally and physically, but she refuses to leave him, or even get help. Every time she calls me crying, every time I see her and she's bruised, I just want to scream because I'm so frustrated, but I'm not sure how far to go in confronting her. I love her more than anything, but I'm afraid if I get tough with her, she'll pull away and be really alone. What should I do?

➡♥♥♥➡ Do *something!* Your friend is in psychological and physical danger, and needs your help *now.* Like many battered women, she may not reach out for help until it's too late. Don't wait for her to ask—she may not even know how. Be a true friend and do everything and anything you can to get her out of this abusive situation, from creating an intervention with other friends and family members, to taking her to a battered women's support group, to getting friends of her husband's to confront him— whatever it takes. (See Question 43.)

Imagine that someone you love is drowning. Your natural impulse is to reach down into the water, grab her arm, and pull her to safety. Would you even have thoughts like *"What if she gets angry with me for pulling hard on her arm? Maybe I shouldn't interfere?"* or

"Maybe if I save her she'll never speak to me again?" Of course not—your only thought would be to save the life of your friend. **Well, your friend is drowning, whether she's aware of it or not. Grab hold of her and pull with everything you have.** So what if she gets angry at first. So what if she flails in her denial for a while. What's important is that you do all you can to get her out of the water before it's too late.

Here's your alternative: One day, you get a call from the hospital informing you that your friend's husband beat her up and she's in intensive care; or one night you're watching television and discover that your friend was murdered by her husband. *How will you feel then? Will it matter that your friend never got mad at you? Will it matter that you "supported" her by not confronting her? I don't think so.*

This is an issue I am passionate about. **If all of us stopped tolerating the mistreatment of our friends, of our friend's children, and anyone we know who is in danger of being harmed in any way, if we spoke out against injustice instead of pretending it wasn't there and hoping it would magically disappear, then perpetrators of violence would not be able to act out their sickness onto others, and the world would be a much safer and kinder place in which to live.**

➡️💕➡️ *SEE ALSO QUESTION 43*

96
How do I deal with the negative influence of my husband's ex-wife on our relationship?

Why didn't anyone tell me when I married my husband that I'd also be marrying his ex-wife? This woman is a nightmare. She is making my husband's life, and therefore mine, totally miserable. She calls him up with screaming fits several times a week; she bad-mouths him to his kids, and makes them feel guilty if they have a good time on their weekends here; and she won't even acknowledge me as his new wife after four years of marriage! I don't want her to win, but I feel like she's poisoning our relationship. My husband claims that there's nothing he can do. How can I keep her from ruining our marriage?

➡❤❤➤ I feel for you. You're describing what I call a *Toxic Ex-Spouse*. Toxic ex-spouses don't respect the boundaries of their relationship with their former wife or husband, and thus, can make your marriage a living hell. Some of the ways they may do this are:

> *They don't respect your privacy.*
> *They use guilt to try and drive a wedge between you and your mate.*
> *They become "time and energy vampires."*
> *They don't acknowledge your relationship.*
> *They financially blackmail your mate by threatening to ask for more money as a way of punishing him/her for being with you.*

They emotionally blackmail your mate by
    threatening to ask for total custody of the
    children.
They turn the children against you or your
    partner.
They come on to your mate sexually as a way to
    interfere.

Toxic ex-spouses are partners who have never really let go of their mates and will hang on for dear life, all the while destroying your relationship. If your partner has a toxic ex-spouse, *you are in an emotional triangle, a threesome.* And don't blame it on the ex. Unless he or she is really mentally ill, your mate is just as guilty by virtue of the fact that he hasn't made his boundaries clear. **If your partner has taken a stand with his ex-spouse, communicated his feelings and set clear boundaries as to what behavior he will accept, you will have much less of a problem regardless of how toxic his ex-spouse may try to be.**

People with toxic ex-spouses have often never completely broken off those relationships. They may still be emotionally married to their ex, and have a difficult time doing anything that would hurt them. Or, it's also possible that your mate *has* let go, but his ex really is disturbed. If this is the case, make sure your partner isn't in denial about his ex's mental problem, and don't accept his excuses like:

"Give her time. She'll get used to it."

"Oh, I know he can be dramatic, but he'd never really do anything to hurt you."

"If we just ignore her, I'm sure she'll stop bothering us."

It sounds like you weren't really aware that this woman was a problem before you got married. That's common—the ex may not start the disturbing behavior until he or she realizes your partner is serious about you. You may also not see how much of a problem it is until you move in with your partner. Perhaps he never told you about the phone calls and visits because he didn't want to upset you. But once you live together, it may become very apparent that his ex is much more in the picture than you believed her to be.

If you are in love with someone who has a toxic ex-spouse it is normal to feel:

- *Angry that your partner seems to be more concerned about his ex's feelings than about yours.*
- *Angry when he accuses you of being jealous instead of understanding how you feel.*
- *Frightened that the problem won't get better with time. (It won't.)*
- *Impatient with his excuses about feeling sorry for his ex.*

- *Suspicious that your mate is using his ex as a way to avoid becoming more intimate with you and going forward in his life. (Quite possible.)*
- *Resentful that your partner never brings you along when he sees his ex, picks up the kids, etc., because he "doesn't want to upset her."*

People like your husband with toxic ex-spouses often have emotional programming that makes letting go of the past very difficult. (See Questions 21, 29, and 84.) Your mate might feel guilty abandoning his ex if one of his own parents left the other. If his parents were divorced, he might identify his ex as his own inner child and feel that rejecting her will make him just like his father who rejected him when he left. *Or he may feel guilty for leaving, and be punishing himself by unconsciously sabotaging his new relationship with you.*

If your partner has a toxic ex-spouse, you must insist that he honor his commitment to you and your marriage by letting go of his ex, relinquishing his responsibility for her, setting boundaries for their relationship and sticking by them. If the problem has been chronic, a period of no contact whatsoever will be necessary. That means the kids go out to the car when he picks them up, and not that he goes in for ten minutes and lets his ex do her number. It means messages are passed in writing or by fax rather than conversation. *It's up to your partner*

to break the pattern. Don't wait for the toxic ex to do it—
she won't.

If you discuss this with your partner, and he repeatedly refuses to confront his ex, you can try suggesting counseling so he can get input from a
professional. If he refuses that, you need to ask yourself why you are letting yourself be treated this way.
Until he makes a complete commitment to you, you
are going to be miserable. Your partner isn't emo-
tionally available because he is still energetically
involved with his ex. Tell him you are leaving, and
to call you when he is finished with his other relationship.

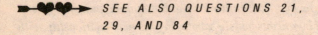 *SEE ALSO QUESTIONS 21,*
29, AND 84

97 *What should you do as a parent when you hate your child's choice of an intimate partner?*

I have always considered myself a tolerant, loving parent to my twenty-four-year-old son who I raised by myself since he was two years old. I've stayed out of his personal life and tried to not force my beliefs about anything on him. But now I'm in a situation that is driving me crazy. My son has a girlfriend who makes my skin crawl! She has no job, no manners, dresses like a tramp, and has pierced every possible place on her body, including some in apparently very private places. Every other word out of her mouth is **#***#* this, and ##**** that, and her idea of a meal is several bottles of beer, a cigarette, and a package of Twinkies. Believe me, I've tried to accept her as she is, but I can't sleep at night thinking about my son involved with her. HELP!!

➤💗💗💗➤ I could give you an enlightened answer such as, *"Inside of this girl is a wounded spirit crying out for help—look beyond her pierced nipples,"* or *"Don't judge a person for what they appear to be on the outside—if she loves your son, that should be all you care about,"* . . . but I won't. Although these sentiments are true from a purely spiritual point of view, in the practical world, I get that she's no one's idea of an ideal daughter-in-law. In fact, she sounds like a nightmare. Yes, she's probably needy, desperate for love, and screaming for attention, but I'm sure you'd rather have her go elsewhere to find it. I don't blame you.

I'm not going to try to psychoanalyze your son as to why he chose this kind of partner, and you shouldn't either. The fact is, for some reason in his life right now, she appeals to him. You and I may strongly suspect (or in your case, pray) that this relationship is going to end badly, but there's no way you are going to convince your son to dump her. *In fact, the more you bad-mouth her, the more rebellious he's going to be.*

The bottom line is this: I think you need to trust your son's character and values, and know that sooner or later, he will get tired of rescuing her, shocking you, punishing himself, or whatever else he's doing, and realize this girl isn't right for him. (Either that or he'll catch his tongue in one of those rings and conclude that continuing to see her may be hazardous to his health.)

In the meantime, you can be supportive to him without being supportive of her. Tell him (as if he doesn't already know) that you are having a hard time totally accepting her, but that . . . (take a deep breath before this next part . . .) you are "glad he's found someone he feels is right for him." *Let him know you want him to be happy, and that above all, you will always there for him, no matter what happens.* This approach will probably take him by surprise and give him the space to have the judgments he expected you to express.

Hang in there. I know you're having frightening visions of grandchildren with pierced navels, but I have a feeling that what you'll end up with will be much more traditional.

98 What do you do about a partner who insists all the problems in the relationship are yours?

I've been living with a man for a little over a year who truly believes that he has no problems, no hang-ups, and no emotional issues from his past. He refuses to hear any feedback from me, or anyone for that matter, about how insensitively he treats people, how impossible he is to talk to, or about any way he might improve as a person. Whenever we argue, which is just about every day, he talks to me in a very condescending manner (he's an attorney!) and insists that I am the only one with problems or faults, and that I need to work on myself to achieve his level of clarity and enlightenment. Do you have any suggestions as to how I can get through to him?

▬━❦❦━➤ Simple . . . follow these instructions carefully. Ready? First, go through every room in your house, open all the drawers, cupboards, and closets and pack all of your clothes and belongings into suitcases and boxes. Next, take out a piece of paper and a pen. Then, write the following note: *"Oh Perfect One, I'm writing to inform you that I finally saw the light and have achieved a new level of clarity and enlightenment. . . . I'm clear that you are an egotistical, narcissistic, dysfunctional human being, and I'm enlightened about the fact that I am leaving you. Thank you for helping me to achieve this state of supreme liberation."*

Leave the note somewhere he is sure to see it. In his case, that's probably a mirror. Then, load up your car, and get the hell out, and don't look back.

99   *Is it normal to feel jealous of the attention my wife gives to the dog?*

This probably sounds like a weird question, but it's a serious problem in my marriage. I think my wife loves our dog more than she loves me. We've had Sparky, a golden retriever, for six years. My wife is always hugging and kissing him, and acts more excited to see him when he walks into the room than she does when I come home from work. As far as my wife's concerned, Sparky never does anything wrong, but she's always complaining about me and how I don't pay attention to her. I try, but Sparky usually gets there first. Naturally, Sparky sleeps with us, or I should say, with my wife on her side of the bed, so I don't even get a chance to have much sex. Is there a solution to this situation?

■━♥♥♥━► I guess the saying "A dog is a man's best friend" doesn't apply in your case, does it? Well, I have the solution: *You need to show your wife you love her in the same way your dog Sparky shows her he loves her.* No, I'm not suggesting you get down on all fours and fetch a tennis ball. But seriously, watch Sparky for a few days and notice how he behaves around your wife:

- *When she walks into a room, he instantly notices, wags his tail wildly and acts like it is a great event.*
- *When he wants some love from her, which is always, he doesn't wait to see if she's in the mood—*

he runs up to her, rubs his body against hers and lets her know he's ready.

- *When your wife comes home, he bounds gleefully to the door and behaves as if he is overjoyed to see her—even if she only went out for two minutes to get the mail.*

- *When your wife is feeling a little down, he never assumes she'll just "get over it," and leaves her alone; instead, he cuddles up even closer to her, just to let her know she is loved.*

- *When your wife gives something to Sparky, whether it's his dinner, a biscuit, a belly rub, or a chew toy, he receives it as if she just blessed him with the greatest gift in the world. He is full of gratitude for the smallest offering.*

- *Sparky never misses an opportunity to give your wife a kiss, a nuzzle, a lick. He never thinks to himself, "I just kissed her an hour ago," or "I'll wait until after dinner." For Sparky any time is the right time for love, the more often the better.*

What you'll see if you watch Sparky is how generously and consistently he adores your wife. He never holds back, he never hides his feelings, he never economizes on his love for her, he never takes her for granted. And in response to this, your wife loves Sparky back in the way you describe. **So it makes sense to me that if you want her to love you**

like that, you have to love her like Sparky does.
Passionately. Devotedly. Twenty-four hours a day.
And without ever worrying about making a fool of
yourself. Woof woof. . . .

100 *Do you believe there is such a thing as a soul mate? Can we have more than one soul mate?*

━━♥♥━━► This is my personal belief and experience—that each of our souls experiences many lifetimes in many different bodies, both male and female, for the purpose of growing in wisdom and love. This progression of experiences develops based on the choices we make in each lifetime, like a personalized cosmic seminar, and particular lessons unfold as needed, some through events, some through circumstances, and many through the other souls we encounter.

In this divine blueprint, everything has a higher purpose, and therefore nothing happens accidentally. And so it is no accident that two particular people come together in a relationship. Out of everyone on the earth, we find one another, sometimes through what appears to be an incredible set of circumstances. Whether we spend a week, a year, or fifty years together, the purpose is the same: *Ultimately, we come together for the purpose of being each other's teacher, and learning everything we can about being a more loving human being.*

Within that great context of our existence, however, there are many kinds of partnerships we can have with a mate along the path toward ultimate liberation. *Sometimes two people are drawn together to work out very intense karma, or emotional and spir-*

itual issues, together. This kind of "karmic workout"
relationship may at times appear to be dramatic,
painful, turbulent, and even unhealthy. It may last a
lifetime, or much less if the couple learns the lessons
quickly enough. But hopefully, when it ends, you've
learned what you were supposed to learn through
your experience with that other person whose issues
perfectly coincided with yours, and you can graduate
to your next level of growth. *Of course, if you choose to*
not learn the lessons, you will have to repeat the class, ei-
ther in the same lifetime with a similar teacher, or in a new
lifetime in a similar situation.

Sometimes, two people are drawn together for
what I call "reminder" or transitional relationships.
These lovers feel like old, dear friends (and they are),
who arrive in your life just when you need a reminder that you are lovable, or that you do deserve
to be treated well, or that you really did want to start
that new business, or that it was time to start taking
better care of yourself. These relationships are like
cosmic alarm clocks, waking you up to a piece of
yourself or your own inner wisdom that you forgot.
The souls who deliver these lovely karmic greeting
cards usually stay for a shorter period of time, moving on to work through their deeper issues with
someone appropriate for them, just as you will. *These*
relationships usually end easily and with love. Their pur-
pose has been fulfilled, and you always feel grateful to have
connected.

Some relationships, many that last a lifetime, are "learning relationships." Two souls come together with very similar assignments, and choose to spend many, many years working through their lessons and helping each other grow. Lasting marriages often fall into this category, especially those that leave both partners with a sense of contentment and peace at the end of their lives. These may not always be the most passionate, intimate love affairs all the time, or the most intensely emotional relationships, but they take each soul to its next level by matching it with another who will create enough safety and support so that it can fulfill the spiritual business it needs to in that particular lifetime.

And then, I believe, there is the relationship between two soul mates, two souls whose destiny is closely connected for all time. Some teachings say that these soul mates are two pieces of a whole separated at the beginning of physical creation; others say that twin souls are the male and female expressions of the same individuation of spiritual energy. **My experience is that a true soul mate is a soul bound to yours by a profound and timeless level of love, trust, and devotion—that its purpose is to help you complete your Journey, as you are to help it complete its Journey.** In the presence of a true soul mate, you grow to feel completely loved, completely safe, completely known, and thus it is easy to remember your true nature as Love, and to make very rapid advancements on the path. It is as if your soul mate reflects back to you the very essence of your soul, and in remembering yourself, you are that much closer to attaining enlightenment.

When you find your soul mate, you feel as if you have always been together, not just in this lifetime, but for all time, and that your reunion fills an intense, eternal longing that has been in your heart until the moment you found each other again, a longing no ordinary relationship can satisfy. Your relationship will still have its challenges, and of course, many lessons, but ultimately, they aren't the predominant focus of your experience. **For every moment that you spend with your soul mate, you are sure of one thing—you have come Home.**

One way to look at relationships is that since, as I believe, we are all part of the same Universal Whole, each partner is a kind of soul mate. Yet my own emotional and spiritual experience and study have revealed to me that there is an enormous difference between the kind of love you feel in these different categories of relationships, and that soul-mate love transcends all the others in a particular way I am still learning to comprehend. Some teachings say that each of us has several of these ultimate soul mates; others indicate that there is only one other soul to which we are connected in this way. Whatever is true, once you are with your soul mate, you will not care if there is another one flying around the Universe somewhere.

This is what is important: *The more committed you are to helping your spirit grow in love, and to learning the lessons you came here this time to learn, the more certain you can be that you will attract the partner who is perfect for you right now. And perhaps, if you are truly blessed, you will discover that your soul mate has come here at this time on earth to travel with you as you Journey Home together.*

Do you have a question to *Ask Barbara*?

Send your letters to:

Barbara De Angelis Corporation
12021 Wilshire Boulevard, Suite 607
Los Angeles, California 90025

And look for more *Ask Barbara* books in the future,
on a wide variety of relationship issues.

Index

© Charles Bush

BARBARA DE ANGELIS, Ph.D., internationally recognized as one of the foremost experts on human relations and personal growth, is the author of seven bestselling books: *The Real Rules, Ask Barbara, Real Moments®, Real Moments® for Lovers, How to Make Love All the Time,* and the #1 *New York Times* blockbusters *Secrets About Men Every Woman Should Know* and *Are You the One for Me?* Her award-winning infomercial airs in hundreds of cities each day and is the most successful program of its kind. She and her husband, Dr. Jeffrey James, live outside Los Angeles.